SANDPAPER ON SUNBURN
DAVID HORAN

Sandpaper on Sunburn was first performed at
Smock Alley Theatre, Dublin, on 26 September 2024
as part of the Dublin Theatre Festival

SANDPAPER ON SUNBURN
by David Horan

Company (in order of appearance)

SONYA	Honi Cooke
TONY PATTISON	Anthony Brophy
FREYA PATTISON	Éilish McLaughlin
COLETTE PATTISON	Amelia Crowley
HELEN PATTISON	Clare Monnelly

Written & Directed by	David Horan
Set & Costume Design	Maree Kearns
Lighting Design	Kevin Smith
Sound Design	Tom Lane
Choreography	Muirne Bloomer
Production Manager	Olivia Drennan
Stage Manager	Aaron Kennedy
Assistant Stage Manager	Susannah Conroy
Chief LX	Síofra Nic Liam
Wardrobe Supervisor	Mairéad O'Brien
Photography	Ros Kavanagh
Producer	Kerry Power
Executive Producer	Donal Shiels

About the Creator
David Horan is a playwright and theatre director living in Dublin.

Cast

Anthony Brophy | Tony

Theatre credits include: *Defender of the Faith* (Decadent Theatre); *Off Plan* (Project); *The Lieutenant of Inishmore* (Town Hall Theatre); *Thesis* (Gúna Núa Theatre Co.); *Last Orders at the Dockside, Observe the Sons of Ulster, Barbaric Comedies, The Plough and the Stars* (Abbey Theatre); *Twenty Grand, Made in China* (Peacock Theatre); *Blue Macushla, Shoot the Crow, The Lonesome West* (Druid Theatre/Royal Court); *Studs, Diarmuid & Grainne* (Passion Machine); *Macbeth, How Many Miles to Babylon* (Second Age Theatre Co.).

Recent screen work includes: *Lady Chatterley's Lover* (Netflix); *FBI International* (Paramount); *Murder in G Major* (Hallmark); *Trial of the Century, Red Rock* (TV3); *The Cherry Tree* (Fantastic Films); *Penny Dreadful, The Informant* (Showtime); Oscar-winning short film *The Shore, CSI* (CBS); *Prime Suspect* (NBC); *Fifty Dead Men Walking* (Brightlight Pictures) and *The Tudors* (CBC/Showtime). Other credits include *In the Name of the Father, Some Mother's Son* (Hell's Kitchen); *Dust* (1I Productions); *The Clinic, Making The Cut* (RTÉ); *The Run of the Country* (Castle Rock); *Mapmaker* (Bandit Films); *Snow White – A Tale of Terror* (Interscope); *The Gathering Storm* (HBO) and *Devil's Own* (Universal).

As a writer, Anthony's first play *Chicane* was shortlisted for the Stewart Parker Award and the Royal Exchange's new writing competition.

His first two novels: *Summer of Stan* and *The Vasectomy Kid!* were both shortlisted for the Irish Writers Centre's 'Novel Fair'.

His short fiction has been published in Irishwritersmagazine.com and The Rose Literary magazine.

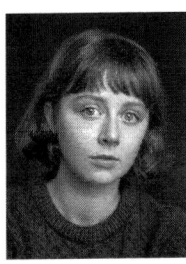

Honi Cooke | Sonya

Honi is from Co. Wicklow. Recent credits include: *Bodkin* (Netflix); *Mayfair Witches* Season 2 (AMC); *Taigh Tŷ Teach* (Fishamble); *On Such As We* (Decadent Theatre at the Wexford Opera House); Viola in *Twelfth Night* (Shakespeare Squared in Waterford's Viking Triangle; winner of Greenroom Award for Best Actress in March '24); and *Tír Na nÓg* (Macalla Teo and RTÉ Jr). She has a BA in Drama and Theatre Studies from Trinity College Dublin, and trained at The Lir Academy, graduating in 2021.

Amelia Crowley | Colette

Amelia is a graduate of Theatre Studies at Trinity College, Dublin.

Theatre credits: *The Cavalcaders* (Druid Production); *Little Gem* (The Bush and Gúna Nua Theatre Company); *Podge and Rodge Live At Vicar Street* (Double Z Productions); *And They Used to Star in Movies* (Bewleys Café Theatre); *The Plough and the Stars* (Abbey/Barbican); *Lucky Sods, Native City* (Tivoli); *Run for your Wife* (national tour); *The Night Garden* (Northcott Theatre); *The Importance of Being Earnest* (Gúna Nua); *Car Show* (Corn Exchange); *Boomtown* (Rough Magic); *Twenty Grand, The Melon Farmer* (Peacock); *Sharon's Grave* (Gate Theatre); *The Broken Jug* (Abbey). Screen credits: *Harry Wild* (Lionsgate); *The Ghost and the Glitch* (Castle Dingle Movie Production); *Derry Girls* (Hat Trick Productions); *Dublin Murders* (BBC/STARZ/RTÉ/EustonFilms); *The Walshes* (Boom Pictures/BBC 4); *The Widower* (NZ Film Productions/ITV); *Val Falvey T.D SITCOM* (Grand Pictures and RTÉ); *This Is Nightlive, Fair City, Stardust, The Clinic, The Cassidys, Upwardly Mobile, Couched, Racing Homer, Finbar's Class* (RTÉ); *Paths to Freedom* (Grand Pictures and RTE); *Val Falvey* (Grand Pictures); *The Wake Wood* (Fantastic Films); *What If* (Bootstrap Films); *Ella Enchanted* (Miramax); *The Halo Effect* (Fastnet Films); *Fergus' Wedding* (Grand Pictures); *Custer's Last Stand Up, I Went Down, Ballykissangel* (BBC); *When Brendan Met Trudy* (Collins Avenue). Radio credits: *Lennon's Guitar, Carry Me Home, The Plough and the Stars* (RTÉ); *Driftwood* (The Write Stuff Productions).

Éilish McLaughlin | Freya

Éilish McLaughlin is a 2019 graduate of The Lir Academy, Dublin. Since graduating she has played an array of roles such as Desdemona in *Othello*, Juliet in *Romeo and Juliet* and Mandy in *Eclipsed* (The Mill Theatre). In 2022 she made her Druid Theatre Company debut in *The Cavalcaders* by Billy Roche, directed by Aaron Monaghan. She also played Fiona in Colette Cullen's *When Rachel Met Fiona* in the New Theatre. She was recently in FourRivers' revival of *A Handful of Stars* by Billy Roche, directed by Conal Morrison, playing the role of Linda.

Her TV credits include a small part in *Rebecca's Boyfriend*, written and directed by Craig Reynolds, and *To Mornington*.

Clare Monnelly | Helen

Clare is an actor and writer from Dublin. As an actor, Clare has worked with Druid, the Abbey, the Gate, Livin' Dred and many more. She has been nominated for three Irish Times Theatre Awards. On screen she has worked with Deadpan Pictures, RTÉ, Sky One and TG4 among others. She recently reprised the role of Anita Fallon in Series 2 of *The Gone* for Keeper Pictures and Kingfisher Films. She plays the lead role of Shoo in Doubleband Pictures and Wildcard's upcoming Irish language horror film *Fréwaka*. She is best known for her roles of Mary in *Nowhere Fast* and Fidelma in *Moone Boy*.

CREATIVE TEAM

David Horan | Writer/Director

David is a playwright and theatre director, Artistic Director of Bewley's Café Theatre and a core Acting Tutor at the Lir National Academy, Dublin.

Credits include: Colm Tóibín's *The Blackwater Lightship* at the Gaiety Theatre (DTF 2022); *CLASS* co-written and directed with Iseult Golden (Edinburgh Fringe First Award). *After Play by Brian Friel* (Bewley's Café Theatre); *This Beautiful Village* by Lisa Tierney-Keogh (Abbey Theatre); *Beowulf: the Blockbuster* by Bryan Burroughs (Edinburgh Fringe Stage Award, IAC New York, NY Times Critic's Pick); *These Halcyon Days* by Deirdre Kinahan (Edinburgh Fringe First Winner/DTF 2012); *Moment* by Deirdre Kinahan (Bush Theatre, London); *Moll* by JB Keane (Gaiety, MCD/Verdant Productions); *Pineapple* by Philip McMahon (Calipo/DTF); *Macbeth, Dancing at Lughnasa* (Second Age); *In The Pipeline* by Gary Murphy (Paines Plough/Òran Mó Theatre, Glasgow); *The Death of Harry Leon by Conall Quinn* (Stewart Parker Award Winner) and the award-winning *Tick my Box!* (Inis Theatre) among others.

Screen credits include *Belonging to Laura*, a contemporary film adaptation of *Lady Windermere's Fan* (Accomplice/TV3) and *The Importance of Being Whatever*, an adaption of *Earnest* (IFTA Winner).

Maree Kearns | Set & Costume Design

Maree is a regular creative collaborator with many of Ireland's leading companies and directors in theatre, dance, opera, and musicals. She has created award winning worlds for performance on stages big and small across the country and internationally, in site-specific locations, immersive experiences and outdoor productions.

Maree's design work has spanned almost two decades and counts set and costume designs for The Abbey & Peacock Theatres, The Ark, Anu Productions, Everyman Theatre, Fishamble Theatre Company, CoisCeim Dance Theatre Company, Cork Opera House, Corn Exchange, An Grianann Theatre, Nomad Theatre Network, Landmark Productions, RIAM, The Lir Academy, Verdant Productions and many more.

Maree has also worked extensively in television and film and is the course director for the Masters in Theatre Design at the Lir Academy in Dublin. She is the recipient of the Tanya Moiseiwitsch Design Award at the Tyrone Guthrie Centre in 2024.

For more information see www.mareekearns.com

Kevin Smith | Lighting Design

Kevin trained at The Samuel Beckett Centre, Trinity College Dublin. He is based in Dublin and has worked in Ireland and internationally designing for theatre, dance and opera.

His previous work with Verdent includes *The Blackwater Lightship*, *Foxy & Moll*. Other theatre work includes *CLASS* (Abbey Theatre & Inis Theatre); *In Two Minds*, *Outrage*, *Spinning* and *Rathmines Road* (Fishamble); *Bang* (Michelle Read); *The Odd Couple* (Everyman Theatre); *Driving Miss Daisy*, *The Snow Queen*, *Aladdin*, *The Little Mermaid*, *Jungle Book* (Gaiety). His opera design credits include *Flight* (Opera Collective); *Die Fledermaus*, *Kiss Me Kate* with NI Opera, *King Arthur*, *Vampirella*, *Saints & Sinners* and *Clori Tirsi é Fileno* (RIAM) and *Flatpack* with Ulysses Opera.

Kevin's dance design credits include *Caged* (Femme Bizarre); *12 Minute Dances* (Liz Roche Co.); *Coppelia* (Ballet Ireland); *Manefesto* (Maiden Voyage).

www.kevinsmith.ie

Tom Lane | Sound Design

Tom Lane is a Dublin-based composer and sound designer. He works frequently to create new music for dance, theatre and opera productions as well as new scores for instrumental and vocal ensembles. Recent work for stage includes music for choreographer Mufutau Yusuf's new work *Impasse* at Dublin Dance Festival, composition for the Olivier Award nominated *The Tragedy of Macbeth* at London's Almeida Theatre directed by Yaël Farber starring Saoirse Ronan, and Erica Murray's *The Loved Ones* directed by Ronan Phelan at The Gate Theatre Dublin. In 2023 his new piece *Nocturne* was performed by the National Symphony Orchestra of Ireland conducted by Gavin Maloney. Tom has previously been commissioned to write new music for the Esker Festival Orchestra, the Picorlino Ensemble, the Banbha Quartet, Cantairí Óga Átha Cliath, Cork Opera House, John Scott Irish Modern Dance Theatre, Northern Ireland Opera, Cantairí Avondale, the Abbey Theatre, the Gate Theatre, Branar Theatre, Kirkos Ensemble, Pipeworks Organ Festival, The Globe Theatre, The Almeida Theatre, and The Ark Theatre.

Muirne Bloomer | Choreography

Muirne Bloomer is from Dublin. She has had an extensive performance career in ballet, contemporary and dance theatre in Ireland and abroad. Muirne has been commissioned by Dublin City Council, Coisceim Dance Theatre, Dublin City Arts Office as well as receiving Arts Council funding for her own original work. Choreography for theatre and opera credits include INO's *La Cenerentola*, nominated for Best Production Irish Times Awards 2020 and the critically acclaimed *Hamlet* for the Gate Theatre in 2019/2020 which transferred to St Ann's Warehouse New York.

Most recently Muirne choreographed Janet Moran's *Quake* for the Dublin Theatre Festival 2023 and Irish National Opera's critically acclaimed production of *La bohème* in the Bord Gais Theatre. Muirne will restage the production with director Orpha Phelan for Le Corum, Montpelier in April/May this year.

Muirne has been a major contributor to large-scale spectacle and pageantry in Ireland and her choreography and staging include: *The World Festival of Families* (Croke Park, 2018); *Laochra* – GAA 2016 Centenary (Croke Park 2016); Opening Ceremony of the UEFA Europa League Final (Aviva Stadium 2011); Ryder Cup (K Club 2007) and Opening Sequence for the Special Olympics (Croke Park 2003).

She is Performance Director for St Patrick's Festival Community Arts and is Artistic Coordinator of Creative Places Darnndale, instrumental in the setting up of the *Made in Darndale* Summer Arts Festival. Muirne frequently guest teaches professional dance class for Irish Modern Dance Theatre and the Introduction to Dance intensive for drama students at the Lir Academy.

Muirne obtained an MA first-class honours in Dance from UL IN 2015 and has just published her book, *In Focus – Dublin City Ballet*, which is based on some of the research from her MA thesis.

Verdant Productions | Producer

Verdant Productions (Producer), formed by Donal Shiels in 2011, produces and promotes a diverse range of live and virtual theatre and music programming in Ireland and internationally. Recent work includes *Mother of All The Behans* adapted by Peter Sheridan from the book by Brian Behan featuring Imelda May (Olympia Theatre); *Falling To Earth* by Eugene O'Brien and *Isla* by Tim Price as part of Dublin Theatre Festival 2023; *Speed The Plow* by David Mamet (Civic Theatre & Pavilion Theatre); *The Blackwater Lightship* by Colm Tóibín adapted by David Horan (Gaiety Theatre) for Dublin Theatre Festival; *Art* by Yasmina Reza (a filmed presentation from The Mill Theatre (Sept 2021), Triskel Courtyard Cork – a three-week programme of outdoor performances in August 2021; *CLASS* by Iseult Golden & David Horan (Irish tour); *A Holy Show* by Janet Moran (Edinburgh Fringe & Project Arts Centre); *Private Peaceful* by Michael Morpurgo (Off Broadway at Barrow Group Theatre & Irish tour); the world premiere of *Copper Face Jacks: The Musical* by Paul Howard (The Olympia Theatre); *My Romantic History* by D.C.Jackson (Irish premiere); *Trainspotting* by Irvine Welsh & Henry Irvine (Olympia Theatre); *The Spinning Heart* by Donal Ryan (Gaiety Theatre); *The Weir* by Conor McPherson (Gaiety Theatre); *Signatories* at Kilmainham Gaol & Olympia Theatre (UCD).

Past work includes Brendan Behan's *Borstal Boy* (Gaiety Theatre); the world premiere of *Anglo the Musical* by Paul Howard (Bord Gáis Energy Theatre); *Hamlet* and *King Lear* by William Shakespeare; *Agrippina* by Handel for Irish Opera Collective (Dublin Fringe Festival); *My Brilliant Divorce* by Geraldine Aaron (Irish tour); *Foxy* by Noelle Brown at Project Arts Centre; *Solpadeine is My Boyfriend* by Stefanie Preissner (Brisbane Powerhouse, Australia); *The Field* by John B Keane with Brian Dennehy, directed by Joe Dowling (Olympia Theatre).

Acknowledgements

Sandpaper on Sunburn received Project Award funding from the Arts Council of Ireland. It was first produced in association with Verdant Productions and the Dublin Theatre Festival in 2024, with the support of the Civic Theatre and Smock Alley Theatre, 1662. The play was initially developed with support from the Pavilion Theatre.

Special Thanks

Willie White, Stephen McManus, Derval Mellet and all at the Dublin Theatre Festival, Lucy Ryan and all at Smock Alley, Donal Shiels, Sandra Doyle and all at the Civic Theatre, Hugh Murray, Dónal Kennedy and all at the Pavilion Artist Studio, David Parnell, Bea Kelleher and all at the Arts Council of Ireland.

The play has had many readers whose time and insights were offered kindly and generously. I'm grateful to Will Irvine, Will O'Connell, Karin McCully, Gerard Stembridge, Stewart Roche, Lisa Tierney-Keogh, Donncha O'Dea, Declan Tarpey, Emma Dargan-Reid, Naoise Dunbar, Aidan Moriarty, Eavan Gaffney, Molly McFadden, Jessie Weaver, Karen Ardiff, Alexandra Conlon, Barry Barnes, Iseult Golden, Colm Maher, Graham Whybrow, Merci Horan, Rachel Horan, and my greatest support, Sarah Ling.

SANDPAPER ON SUNBURN

David Horan

For Joe Horan

Characters

SONYA (SON [*rhymes with 'on'*]), *Freya's ex, twenty-three*
TONY (TONE) PATTISON, *Freya's dad, fifties*
FREYA PATTISON, *twenty-four*
COLETTE (COLLIE) PATTISON, *Freya's mam, fifties*
HELEN (HELS) PATTISON, *Freya's sister, twenty-nine*

Note on Text

A forward slash (/) indicates when the next line starts before the current line is finished.

Text in [square brackets] indicates the end of a line or a thought that is not said.

This text went to press before the end of rehearsals and so may differ slightly from the play as performed.

ACT ONE

Music. Something like 'First Prize Bravery' by Sorcha Richardson. Upbeat, contemporary, the female voice of a generation.

The full cast assembles a living room in a make-and-do, fun sort of way. This is the Pattisons' living room.

When a wall/flat is put in position, a projection:

'2018'

Projections and music fade/cut.

SONYA *is standing and* TONY PATTISON *is on the couch.*

A silence.

TONY. It's been a mad day. Just... mad.

Beat.

Everyone's up to here, you know? High doh.

I'm sure she'll... [come back] in her own time – you know yourself.

But you'll wait. Sit. It's no bother. You're welcome, Sonya. Always are, you know that.

SONYA *sits.* TONY *stands.*

Now. I'll get you something, a drink or – ?

SONYA. High doh?

TONY. Oh, for Jack. He's four. We had a thing for him.

SONYA. A party?

TONY. Just family. He doesn't have many friends, he's four. So Colette and I offered. To take the pressure off Helen. And for... Freya too. We thought it might be good to make a fuss.

SONYA (*deliberately*). Freya, is she –

TONY. Yeah, yeah. She's ehm… She's great.

How are you anyway? It's been a while.

SONYA. I'm good. Thanks, Mr Pattison – … Tony.

Beat.

TONY. Do you need anything or…?

SONYA. Just. To talk.

TONY. Right, yeah… Will I call her? (*Unsure.*) Do you think?

TONY *goes and calls*.

Frey? Freya, Sonya wants to talk to ya? FREYA!

A silence.

TONY *shrugs at* SONYA, *resigned*.

Perhaps it's something I can…? No actually, best leave me out of it. I don't want to get into more trouble.

Not that I'm taking sides.

Well I am. She's my daughter. Of course I'm on her side.

Beat.

But we're all adults now… and things don't always work out… and no one's to blame. We know that, Sonya.

Sure isn't it what you wanted? To be like the rest of us. To be able to get married or, call it a day. Because it's all part of it.

And it's not like Freya's ever been, easy.

What am I saying, sure you know better than –

SONYA. I just, want to talk.

TONY. Right-o, well. Sit tight.

TONY *sits*.

She's bound to… resurface.

Beat.

SONYA. Looks the same. The house.

TONY. Yeah? Sure why wouldn't it? Oh except for the –

ACT ONE   7

SONYA. Solar panels.

TONY. Outside, yeah, you saw them? We get more light on the front. I'd have preferred the back but the angle – they look all right though?

SONYA (*nodding*). Doing your bit.

TONY. That's it.

The lads down the garage helped install them so... not too expensive. Almost looking forward to the leccy bill.

SONYA. You'll be making money.

TONY. Wouldn't go that far... How is it the ad goes? 'Every little helps'?

Cos you think, y'know, when they finish college and finally they're out, taking care of themselves – like I was sixteen when I started working – so you think right, maybe now we can, relax. Colette and me, we can actually... But it never stops...

SONYA. You okay, Tony?

TONY. Mad day.

Beat.

SONYA. Freya will be pleased.

(*Off* TONY*'s confusion.*) With the solar panels.

TONY. Oh yeah. Cartwheels.

SONYA. And is there a car to work on?

TONY. Always.

SONYA. What this time?

TONY *takes out his phone and shows* SONYA *pictures on it.*

TONY. Sky-blue 1970s Ford Consul.

Doing it as a favour. Some rust around the wheel arches, and the brakes need looking at. But good condition.

Ah, she's a beaut. You wanna see this engine. Proper workmanship. A family car, not like the coupé – that came later. Tell you what, if you're interested... drop down the workshop some evening, week after next, she'll be ready. I'll bring you for a spin.

Beat.

SONYA. It is nice to see you.

TONY (*moved*). Ah here. Of course it is.

(*Tenderly.*) It's great to see you. Sure we all miss ya. Colette. Helen. Me. And Freya. You know that.

Beat.

SONYA. You're in trouble…

(*Off* TONY*'s look.*) You said. You don't want to get into more trouble.

TONY. Oh that. God, don't remind me…

FREYA *enters*.

FREYA. Tony hit Jack. Slapped his only grandson.

TONY. Excuse me, I did not.

FREYA. We all saw it.

TONY (*to* SONYA). Jack was getting too close to the candles. I was protecting him.

FREYA. By slapping him?

TONY. He bit me, the little bastard.

SONYA. Mr Pattison!

TONY (*to* SONYA, *re:* FREYA). Now don't be listening to how she puts it. She makes everything sound worse than it is.

FREYA. Who's she? The cat's mother.

TONY. Sonya, I'm sorry, I shouldn't have used that word about Jack but…

He is fascinated by candles. You know how kids are. Jack blows out the candles, we all cheer, he wants to do it again. So we do. And we do. And we do, I don't know how many times and I'm relighting these things each and every – you know, next year we should get the ones, you know those candles that light back up by themselves? Jack would love that.

Anyway, the yoke, the lighter thingy, is scorching my hand, so I'm struggling. And the little fella's getting more and more excited, leaning in, all ready to blow. But I can't physically see the cake any more. I can't see what I'm doing!

So I go to move him back and the little... skite goes and bites me. Look, there's still a mark.

So I push him – no, I don't push him. I pat him. Gently. Not in retaliation – though it bloody hurt! – more to let him know not to be biting people.

And he loses it. And then his mother loses it. I don't know which is worse.

But this only makes the lad even more upset and before you can say 'For he's a jolly good fellow', we're in full-blown, nuclear territory and nothing will calm the situation... In the end his granny has to go and offer to drop them both off at his father's. Nothing for it. Bleedin' disaster.

And all because of the candles.

FREYA. It must have been more than a pat, Dad. The child freakin' lost it.

TONY. He gets tantrums, Sonya. Like this one when she was younger. And not that much younger, as I'm sure you know.

FREYA. Helen couldn't get Jack to calm down. And she was having a drink because the whole idea was to give Hels a break for the day so... No car! Mam had to do the honours. No chance of Jack getting in a car with Granddad. Nice one, Tony.

TONY. Ah jays... Anyway...

Beat.

I will leave you two. To talk.

FREYA. No.

Tense pause.

TONY. Ah no, I will. I'm sure you've got loads to catch up on.

FREYA (*to* SONYA, *forcefully*). Why are you here?

Beat.

SONYA. Mary Robinson's been found. Not found. Sighted.

FREYA. When?

SONYA. I got a call from a woman. She saw her this morning. She was on her way to the shops and she saw Mary Robinson.

FREYA. Where?

SONYA. The Harold's Cross area.

FREYA. Could she be more exact?

SONYA. She hadn't her mobile with her. Or the flyer. So she called when she got home. She's convinced it's her, Frey.

Beat. FREYA *folds her arms.*

I thought you would want to know.

FREYA. Was it Loretta?

SONYA. Sorry?

FREYA. This woman who called. Is her name Loretta?

SONYA (*surprised*). Yes!

FREYA. Yeah. She called before.

SONYA. She called…? No she didn't.

FREYA. The woman's batshit.

SONYA. When? When did she call?

FREYA. Three months ago. When Mary Robinson first went [missing] – … Loretta called three months ago.

SONYA. She called you?

FREYA. My number's on the flyer as well. Or don't you remember?

TONY. Can I just check, we are talking about the cat, yes? Not the former president / of –

FREYA. Of course, Dad. We're talking about our cat. But somehow when we broke up, she became Sonya's cat.

ACT ONE   11

SONYA. That's not what happened.

FREYA. And you couldn't look after her for – what was it? – not even a whole month before Mary Robinson ran away? Probably went looking for me. But did she find me, Sonya, did she?

SONYA. Well maybe now. That's why I'm here. Loretta says –

FREYA. Yes?

SONYA. She'll bring her mobile with her next time she goes out and if she sees Mary Robinson she'll take a photograph and then we'll have proof.

But if we want, we can go round there now.

I can go by myself but I thought, if we did it together it could be... healing, sort of.

Imagine we found her, after all this time. Don't you think?

Beat.

FREYA. The woman's out of her mind.

TONY. Freya!

FREYA *(drily)*. Child-beater?

TONY. Hey!

FREYA. Joke. Just a joke.

TONY. Well it's not funny.

FREYA. And neither is an old woman preying on a broken-hearted cat lover, just to give some kind of meaning to her day.

SONYA. She's not doing that.

FREYA. I remember her. Loretta. Complete doolally. How can you be taking this seriously, Son?

SONYA. You don't have to come.

FREYA. I won't come.

SONYA. Really?

Finding Mary Robinson could help, Freya. You're still angry, obviously. And it can be good, to put that somewhere. To take action. Even if we don't – [find her.]

FREYA. I am taking action. Tell her, Dad.

Beat.

What I've been doing.

TONY. ... Oh. Right. Well you see, Sonya, while Freya's been staying here, as I understand it, she's been... well, she's been online. A lot.

FREYA. Thanks, Tony. Super-helpful.

Look, I may be kidding myself, Sonya. I probably am. But I'm trying to work more independently, if I can. There's all this political energy out there right now, this really positive, people feel they can actually change things. So I thought, if I can – I don't know – find a way of... helping. Consulting. On the legal stuff.

And I know how that sounds. Like I'm only starting out and this involves relationship building, not my strong suit, frankly – I'm better at turning people off – case in point, us, I know, it's quite the saviour complex I've got going here – but I think I might actually be... helping. There's these community leaders talking to me. Proposed legislation. Implementation. They have this mad idea I can help, they're the ones calling it a movement – and honestly, Sonya, no one's more surprised than me. But I'm inundated so...

I don't have time for wild goose chases in Harold's Cross. Wild cat chases, whatever.

SONYA. That sounds great, Freya.

FREYA. It's... really fucking hard actually but...

SONYA. I'm glad you're doing better. Because I did worry. About you.

I never meant to... I mean, we both, hurt each other, so.

Beat.

I'm sorry, Tony.

ACT ONE   13

TONY. No, Sonya, that's very mature of you.

FREYA. Shut up, Dad.

TONY. Freya.

FREYA. Don't indulge this, this –

SONYA (*fighting back*). This what?

FREYA. This victim mentality. Feel sorry for me. It's pathetic.

You know well, Sonya, this woman must have seen any ginger cat. Yet somehow she has so little going on in her life she remembers a flyer posted to a lamp post THREE MONTHS AGO, and she's so convinced it's our cat she'll ring you with no evidence whatsoever – no street name, no photo?

It's mental. Do you not see how mental it is?

Someone has to say it.

SONYA. Okay, Freya. Thanks.

FREYA. For what?

SONYA. For being you.

FREYA. You could have called.

You could have called me. You didn't have to come here.

SONYA. I thought we would go together.

FREYA. A simple phone call –

SONYA. You blocked me. Don't you remember? You blocked my number.

Beat.

FREYA. Oh yeah.

SONYA. Yeah… so… I think I'll – [let myself out.]

FREYA. Yep…

Beat.

SONYA. Okay…

See you, Tony.

TONY. Bye, Sonya.

SONYA *turns to go.*

FREYA. This woman's taking advantage. She's lonely so she'll say, anything. It's sad but… I'm only trying to look out for you, Sonya. Like always.

SONYA. You don't have to. Not any more.

FREYA. This isn't me bulldozing.

SONYA. It's not?

FREYA. Maybe it is. But you said… you said you like when I stick up for you, speak up for you –

SONYA. And I did.

FREYA. – I'm your warrior princess.

This last line has slipped out. They both look at TONY, *who coughs. Then, they smile.*

Look, I'm an eejit. I was shocked, to see you. I don't know why I react like –

SONYA. It's okay. Loretta is… unreliable. I do know that but –

FREYA. You won't find Mary Robinson.

SONYA. Still though. I have to try.

SONYA *is about to leave when the front door is heard.* COLETTE *enters.*

COLETTE. Sonya! You're here, love. Well isn't this a nice surprise?

SONYA. I was just leaving, Colette.

FREYA. She was leaving, Mam.

COLETTE. Ah no. No! Stay for a bit. Sure we haven't seen ya.

SONYA. I have to get going. Sorry.

TONY. She's after Mary Robinson.

COLETTE (*barring* SONYA*'s way*). What's that?

TONY. The cat. There's been a sighting.

COLETTE. Oh, well isn't that wonderful news? After so long!

FREYA. It's a hoax, Mam.

COLETTE. A hoax?

FREYA. The whole cat situation… – Look, don't worry about it, how's Jack doing?

COLETTE. Oh, he's fine now. Calmed down before we even got to his father's. Plonked himself by his Lego as if nothing had happened. A little angel again. Well, he's no angel… but is it any wonder? What must it be like for him? Shunted about the place, over and back. And I know he's picking up on everything that's going on. Gary was only delighted to see us, you can imagine. Helen all apologies.

When they're that age all a child wants is routine, but this year? One upheaval after another for poor Jack. So he gets cranky. Or a little more than cranky. But do you blame him? He's such a clever boy. He knows what's happening. It's no wonder today was too much for him.

(*To* TONY.) Helen wanted to stay with him so I left her there. At Gary's! And Gary's mother visiting? I don't know. Helen's not quite herself if you ask me.

Did you hear about all the commotion, Sonya?

SONYA *nods*.

Tony, I was mortified.

TONY. Ah give over, it's not like it's the first tantrum we ever saw.

COLETTE (*looking at* FREYA). Of course not.

But we wanted to give Helen a break from all that. Mothers these days. They need to have more grit about them. Not give in so easily to bad moods.

I wonder how he gets on at his father's. Though he seemed happy there now.

(*To* SONYA.) You remember Gary?

FREYA. Of course she remembers Gary, Mam. She was at their wedding!

COLETTE. Oh of course you were!

FREYA. And the hen.

COLETTE. Yes, thank you, Freya.

FREYA. And Jack's christening.

COLETTE. Freya, please – !

FREYA. Just saying.

COLETTE. Anyway, Sonya, little Jack has been acting up ever since the separation. It's hard on the children.

FREYA. Not to mention the grandparents.

(*To* SONYA.) Two martyrs we have here. One daughter getting a divorce and the other moves back home in her twenties. Talk about cramping their style. Just when Tony was dreaming of motor engines. And Mam booking mini-breaks to Torremolinos.

COLETTE. It is lovely there this time of year. When I was an air hostess, Sonya, I adored the Mediterranean in the autumn. Have you ever been?

SONYA *shakes her head*.

FREYA. I ruin everything. We're complete failures, Helen and I, aren't we, Mother?

COLETTE. We were only thinking about going to Torremolinos. And we didn't want to abandon Helen is the truth of it.

(*To* FREYA.) I thought you were revamping your life. A renaissance, she's taken to calling it. Starting a movement from her boxroom. It's all very exciting.

FREYA. It is, actually.

COLETTE (*to* SONYA). Anyway, sit, Sonya. How have things been for you?

FREYA. Oh yes, don't mind me. The woman who broke my heart is only standing in our living room, but don't mind me.

COLETTE. I'm trying to have a conversation with Sonya now, Freya. If you don't mind.

FREYA. Serious?

COLETTE. Serious. I've had it up to here with tantrums. We last saw Sonya – when was it? Gosh. The day of the celebrations!

TONY. Dublin Castle. We went for that drink.

COLETTE. That's right, that's the last time – ! And you were so happy. (*A touch patronising.*) For the women of Ireland! I am not a vessel! Remember your sign?

FREYA. Mam!

COLETTE. And you were going on and on. You won by that much you couldn't credit it.

'They're finally treating us like proper citizens.' Remember your toast, Sonya, 'To Women, taking their rightful place in Irish society.'

FREYA. Eh, I think that was me.

COLETTE. And we could see it. Like a... sheen. Coming off you. Both so... beautiful, you were... luminous... Luminously happy. And so happy together, remember, Tony?

Beat. SONYA *and* FREYA *embarrassed by each other.*

'The old Ireland is gone.' You had your face painted.

SONYA. Did I?

COLETTE. And then what? A couple of weeks go by, kaput!... What happened?

This break-up of yours affects us all, you know. Just like with Gary. We miss you, Sonya. I miss you. (A lot more than I miss Gary.) The whole family miss you.

Now did Tony offer you something?

FREYA. Unbelievable.

FREYA *exits. They all absorb it.*

TONY. You'll have tea. How is it you take it again – no milk, right?

SONYA. No thank you.

COLETTE (*to* SONYA, *re:* FREYA). She isn't coping.

SONYA. I... I ought to go.

COLETTE. Freya misses you.

TONY. Collie, leave her be. She has a cat to save.

SONYA. I didn't mean for any –

COLETTE. She's always been so active. You know Freya. Always on the go, five conversations at once. More energy than is good for her. But now she hardly leaves that room upstairs. She's not eating. Not eating well at any rate. Sleeping in. She says she's working half the night but it's not like her, is it, Tone? And then there's her actual job.

TONY. This isn't Sonya's problem, Colette.

COLETTE. I know. I know that. I just wanted you to know, Sonya. (*To* TONY.) I'm sure she's interested.

SONYA. My mam called me –

COLETTE. Oh how is she, poor thing?

SONYA. She's okay, yeah. She's pretty, stable these days. They've got a good balance on her meds now. She's in Galway so she calls. I can't go to her right now because I've, you know, responsibilities in Dublin.

Anyway, I was speaking to her the other week and she said I can be hard to – I'm not always the most, expressive person. And she says that's fine except it's hard to know what I want sometimes. What I want from people. I suppose she means it's hard to know what I want from her. Which I don't think is much, actually.

Beat.

Maybe it's the same with Freya. If she's less outgoing just right now, it's understandable, all things considered... so it's okay to, allow that. For now.

ACT ONE 19

COLETTE. If you think so.

SONYA. I'm sorry. I feel really bad...

COLETTE. Of course you do.

SONYA. ...That I lost Mary Robinson. I feel bad about that. I love Mary. And I know it's probably not her that that woman saw but... If there's a chance.

TONY. We know, love.

COLETTE is confused. FREYA enters again.

FREYA (*direct to* SONYA). Take me back.

Pause. Then she tries humour...

Don't leave me here with these two nutters.

No, I'm serious.

I'm getting a real handle on things, Sonya. And if you think about it, we tried being apart and it's not working. Let's try to be together again.

We could take it slow. A trial period.

SONYA. I came because of Mary Robinson.

FREYA. And Doolally in Harold's Cross, I know but...

Our cat is dead, Sonya. We don't have to be.

SONYA. It isn't working for you.

FREYA. What?

SONYA. How do you know being apart isn't working for me?

FREYA. Because... I... Well...

Beat.

(*Almost defeated, then...*) You found this flimsy excuse to come see me.

(*With conviction.*) Because you love me. You love me more than you love Mary Robinson.

SONYA. I really love Mary Robinson.

FREYA. I know you do. We all do. That's why we called her, Mary Robinson.

It's been four months.

Pause.

SONYA. I'm just not sure...

FREYA. What?

SONYA. I'm not sure time was our problem.

Beat.

FREYA. It's because I don't listen.

COLETTE. You don't listen.

TONY. Collie!

FREYA. I'm so busy doing my thing, I don't always see... your... [thing.]

And when you complain, I need to let you, and not try to fix everything all the time. Even if the complaining drives me fucking insane.

COLETTE. Language.

TONY. Collie!

FREYA. And I'll stop being so sarcastic. Even if I can be excellent at sarcasm, there are other modes of communication – it doesn't have to be my default setting.

You see I always have a plan for the day. And you don't – often don't – have any plans, Sonya. But that doesn't mean we have to do what I want just because I'm the one who makes plans. Because that's not fair. I see that now. I do.

And I know I'm not always very... tactile. But I have to let you be tactile, when you need to be. Because otherwise I have all the power on a physical level. And if I believe in equality – and you know I believe in equality – well if I believe in equality then that belief should extend at least as far as our own bedroom.

Beat.

You see, I listen. I have listened. The first thing is to recognise there's a problem and then you can start fixing it. I've had four months. I recognise the problem.

Beat. TONY *and* COLETTE *are looking at* FREYA. *Astonished.*

Sonya?

TONY *and* COLETTE *look at* SONYA.

SONYA. I have to use the bathroom.

SONYA *exits hurriedly.* COLETTE *sinks, dejected.* TONY *watches* FREYA, *who remains suspended.*

FREYA. Well what the fuck does that mean?

COLETTE. Language, Freya!

TONY. You put it out there.

FREYA. What do you think?

TONY. It's the best any of us can do. Say what you feel, what you really feel and if people can't handle it, or the world doesn't want to hear it, you keep on being you, Freya Pattison.

FREYA. Thanks, Dad.

COLETTE. Only…

FREYA. What?

TONY. Yeah, what?

COLETTE. Freya's pretty good at, you know, being herself. Being a bit less herself is what she was talking about. If you listen to Sonya's actual complaints.

FREYA. I have listened.

COLETTE. It's your father I'm disagreeing with.

FREYA. You sure?

COLETTE. Will she be long, do you think? Why doesn't she stay for tea? And cake! Jack's birthday cake. She'll have a slice. Get her to stay, Freya.

(*To* TONY.) Help me.

TONY. Right-o.

FREYA. I can't make her…

> TONY *follows* COLETTE *out.*

…stay. If only…

(*To herself, pacing, choosing her words with difficulty.*) Sonya, Son… I don't know why things got so strained between us but I reckon I was… I didn't know how to… be… what you… wanted. Oh Jesus!

> FREYA *is upside down on the couch as* HELEN *enters from the hallway.* HELEN *jumps when she sees her.*

HELEN. Ohmygod!

Beat.

Mam not here? Or Dad?

FREYA. Hi Freya, how are you?

HELEN. You're dressing again. That's something.

FREYA. You're single again. That's something.

HELEN. So are you. That's a ridiculous thing to say.

FREYA. I know, I'm ridiculous.

HELEN. Where's Mam and Dad?

FREYA. Kitchen.

> HELEN *heads for the kitchen. She is stopped by…*

Sonya's here.

HELEN. What?

FREYA. She's in the bathroom. I've to get her to stay. Mam and Dad will be in with some tea, and cake.

HELEN. Oh that cake! At least it'll get eaten, I suppose. (*With interest.*) Is Sonya back then?

FREYA. What you mean?

HELEN. Are you two... you know...?

FREYA. We'll see.

HELEN. Oh good. Frey. That's good.

FREYA (*like a teenager*). Yeah, well.

HELEN *doesn't know what to make of this response.*
COLETTE *enters with cake and side plates.*

COLETTE. Well, is she staying? Your father's bringing in the tea now – Helen?

HELEN. Hi Mam, I got Gary to drop me back over.

COLETTE. What about Jack?

HELEN. Gary's mam. He's all right with her. She can cope.

COLETTE. Not like your father. I didn't know you were planning on –

HELEN. No, I know. I just...

I hear Sonya's back.

COLETTE. Is she still in the bathroom? Will she have cake?

FREYA. I haven't asked her yet, have I?

COLETTE. Well there's plenty to share. Your father'll get a plate for you, Helen.

(*To* FREYA.) Get me a chair.

(*Calling out.*) Tony? Bring an extra plate for Helen.

(*To* FREYA, *impatient*.) We'll need another chair.

TONY *enters with tea on a tray.*

TONY. What's that? Oh Helen, I didn't know you were coming back.

HELEN. Gary dropped me over.

COLETTE. She'll need a plate.

TONY (*leaving down the tray*). Be right back.

FREYA (*returning with a chair*). I hope she hasn't fallen in.

COLETTE (*initially confused*). Who?

Oh Sonya. Poor thing. She might be a bit emotional.

HELEN. Really? Why?

COLETTE. Well… because Freya –

FREYA. Mary Robinson's been found.

HELEN. Has she?

FREYA. No. Long story.

TONY *is back with an extra plate and mug.*

TONY. Will I pour?

COLETTE. Do, love. We'll all have tea.

COLETTE *slices cake.*

And pour one for Sonya too. She has been a while.

TONY (*pouring*). Is Jack feeling better? Your mother said he calmed down at Gary's.

HELEN. Yeah, he's fine now. I'm sorry about earlier, Dad.

TONY. No, no, I shouldn't have been so forceful with him.

HELEN. You weren't really.

COLETTE. He was. He's too rowdy.

FREYA (*ribbing*). He hit him.

TONY. I never hit him. I patted him, gently, for his own safety.

COLETTE. Jack's a sensitive boy, and Tony should have known better.

HELEN. No, Mam –

TONY. I should have, Helen. I'm sorry for all the kerfuffle. And on his birthday.

COLETTE. I shouldn't have a slice, but I'm going to after all the stress. What is Sonya doing in there, Freya?

FREYA. I can't bloody well go in and ask her!

TONY. Have you heard a flush?

COLETTE. Jesus, Tony!

Beat.

I thought you were going to go on home, Helen.

HELEN. Yeah I got Gary to drop me back because I need to explain something to you, about Jack. Something happened during the week.

COLETTE. What's that?

SONYA enters, sheepish.

Oh Sonya, we're having tea. And Jack's birthday cake. You'll have a slice.

HELEN. Hi Sonya.

SONYA. Helen. Is Jack – ?

HELEN. He's at Gary's.

TONY. So we'll eat his cake in honour of him. Will you join us, Sonya?

SONYA looks at FREYA.

FREYA. Carbs and caffeine. Impossible to resist, right?

SONYA (*choosing to sit*). I can't stay long.

TONY. Stay as long as you like.

COLETTE. We mean that. You're always welcome.

FREYA. Go easy, guys.

SONYA (*to* HELEN). I didn't know it was his birthday. I would have brought a present.

HELEN. Don't be silly.

TONY. Dig in.

COLETTE. Do. Everyone!

Everyone has their tea and cake. There's a small hiatus because the cake is sickly sweet. Initial 'mmm's and 'ah's turn to awkward silence. No one likes it.

HELEN. It's very sweet, isn't it?

COLETTE. Well, it is for a four-year-old.

TONY. There's a lot of icing.

FREYA. It's, like, fifty per cent icing.

HELEN. He'd be up the walls. Where did you buy it, Mam?

COLETTE. What do you think, Sonya? I got it in Smyth's bakery. It is sweet.

SONYA. It's a little dry.

HELEN. It's sticking to the roof of my –

TONY. Wash it down with the tea.

FREYA. It's fucking awful is what it is.

COLETTE. Language, Freya!

All, except COLETTE, *laugh. Even* SONYA *smiles.*

I bought it for the design.

HELEN. Is it stale?

TONY. Something gone-off about it.

FREYA. It's a funny kind of a texture, like a...

SONYA. Chewy...

TONY. Gluey...

HELEN. Plastic?!

FREYA. Christ! Nobody eat another bite!

TONY. Lucky Jack! Escaped having to stomach his awful birthday cake. His granny was out to poison him all along. It was a blessing! Anyone for more tea?

A chorus of 'Yes please's and hands in the air.

I'll fill the kettle.

TONY *exits*.

FREYA. / Thanks, Tony.

HELEN. / Thanks, Dad.

ACT ONE 27

COLETTE. Thanks, love.

This day? One disaster after another.

SONYA. Hopefully not.

COLETTE. That's right. Hopefully not.

FREYA (*to* SONYA). Are you really going to look for her in Harold's Cross?

COLETTE (*mouthing to* HELEN). The cat!

HELEN *nods*.

SONYA. I should get going.

FREYA. I might come with you. Help with the search?

SONYA. Really?

FREYA. Two eyes are better than one, or. But we shouldn't get our hopes up.

SONYA. I know, yeah. Sure!

COLETTE. Let's have some more tea first.

HELEN. Wash that awful stuff down. After Mam trying to kill us.

COLETTE. Tony won't be long with a hot drop.

SONYA. Okay.

A happy hiatus.

HELEN. About Jack…

COLETTE. Your father feels terrible about this morning.

HELEN. He doesn't have to.

COLETTE. You got upset yourself, you remember.

FREYA. You went off on him.

HELEN. Thanks, Freya, I was there.

And I'm sorry but… I suppose, I'm not at my best right now, either, dealing with…

COLETTE. …What?

HELEN. This news about Jack. Well, sort of news.

TONY *enters with a new pot of tea.*

COLETTE. What news about Jack?

TONY. There's news about Jack?

HELEN (*irked*). I've been trying to tell you.

COLETTE. Have you?

HELEN. Yes! Since I arrived. I've been trying to tell you both.

TONY. Sorry, Hels. We didn't realise.

HELEN. It's okay. It's not... It's fine.

Pause.

FREYA. Well go on so.

HELEN. Gary says I have to tell you, but it makes it... very real.

I wanted to wait for a... you know, for a proper, diagnosis. But after today...

COLETTE. Diagnosis?

Beat.

HELEN. I was dropping Jack to playschool Tuesday and I was already late but Miss Gloria – you know the one Jack likes – Miss Gloria asks if I can hang on, go down to the office. For a chat. And we sit there in silence, waiting for Mrs Kelly. She has kids' drawings plastered on every wall – it should be cute but... Anyway, Mrs Kelly finally arrives in. Thanks me for waiting, says she knows how busy I am. (Which I suspect is a dig.) And then she declares that she's worried! About Jack, about his development. And had I noticed anything?

Had I noticed anything. I mean... I know I work but what kind of mother does she – ...

Beat.

You see, we thought it was because of Gary moving out – Jack's moods. How picky he is now with his food. This last year he's been so difficult – (*Referencing* TONY.) as you know. According to Mrs Kelly, Jack may be finding certain things 'harder to process'. And that could be the root cause of his... his bad form. He's only started there a few weeks, but already they've noticed he prefers to play on his own. And his eye contact's not great.

TONY. And from that, they're saying – ...?

HELEN. Not just that. They asked a lot of questions about him.

FREYA. Like what?

HELEN. Like... Can he go quiet for a long time? And not respond to his name when I call him? Has he 'obsessive interests'? And, of course, they knew some of the answers already.

Getting upset.

She asked me does he ever avoid physical contact?

COLETTE. Oh Helen!

HELEN. And you know how he hates to be surprised when you touch him, like today with Dad. It may be it's overstimulating for him if he is... and it may be mild, but it might not be, so we'll get him to see someone soon because we have to know.

She cries.

I'm sorry, Sonya.

SONYA. God, no, Helen. I'm sorry.

Beat.

HELEN. It is possible that it's nothing. That we're all overreacting. Mrs Kelly did say that.

TONY. Really?

HELEN. We don't know.

Pause.

COLETTE (*to* SONYA). Jack's a clever boy. And he talks quite a lot. He'd talk your ears off sometimes, if you'd let him.

HELEN. Obsessively, you mean?

COLETTE. No. No, I mean Jack can be sensitive. His intelligence makes him impatient. So he lashes out.

FREYA. Not helping, Mam.

COLETTE. Starting school is a difficult transition for any child. I remember the two of you in playschool. Especially Freya. She hated it.

FREYA. Mam.

COLETTE. Do you remember, Tony? Freya barred all the other kids from playing with the toy farm. She had no problem standing up for herself even then.

HELEN. What's that got to do with anything?

COLETTE. Just that Jack's allowed to be overwhelmed. He'll settle down, I'm sure of it.

HELEN. Let's hope.

Beat.

COLETTE. What's Gary saying?

HELEN. He wanted me to tell you.

COLETTE. I bet.

Beat.

(*To* SONYA.) Gary's an accountant. They like to keep score.

HELEN. Mam!

COLETTE. Well is it any wonder his child likes having things in order?

HELEN. And I'm in insurance. How / does that – [affect Jack?]

COLETTE. All of that family can be a little bit –

TONY. Collie!

COLETTE. Snobby! – Is what I was going to say. They'll blame us. Wait till you see.

FREYA. For what? You just said Jack's fine.

COLETTE. And he is. Of course, he is.

HELEN. I'm trying to think about Jack right now and what he needs.

Pause.

COLETTE. I'm sorry for what I said about Gary. I didn't mean it. I'm just a little thrown.

HELEN. You're thrown.

TONY. You must have got a terrible shock, when she said it to you.

HELEN. Honestly, I think I'm still in shock.

FREYA. What does Jack need?

HELEN. Well he has to be assessed and there's a waiting list. That's as far as I've got.

FREYA. I'm happy to go with you to any appointment, Hels. I'm not doing the nine-to-five at the moment so.

COLETTE. No… she's not.

FREYA ignores the judgement in this.

FREYA. Just if you need to talk to the specialist or whatever, and have someone else look after Jack.

COLETTE. I'm sure Gary will go with her.

HELEN. Yes… probably.

COLETTE. I don't know why we have to put labels on everything these days.

FREYA. Not a label, Mam.

COLETTE. It's simply a way for the school to pass the problem back to the parent.

FREYA. Still not a label.

COLETTE. Well what is it then?

FREYA. I'm gay. Are you calling that a label?

COLETTE. That's a different issue.

FREYA. Not an issue, Mam. And not a label. Careful though, because you just 'labelled' Jack 'a problem for the school' there.

COLETTE. I did not.

FREYA. She's sorry, Helen. She didn't mean it.

COLETTE. Of course I didn't mean it. Helen knows well what I mean.

I don't want it to snowball into something it's not.

TONY. I can't see it turning out to be that big of a deal. Sure he's a great lad, Jack.

HELEN. Yeah.

COLETTE. Absolutely. I'm convinced it'll be nothing. Nothing at all.

FREYA. But if it was… something, whatever. We'd all be okay with it. Right, Mam?

COLETTE. What do you mean?

FREYA. It wouldn't be the end of the world.

COLETTE. Of course not. Sure we all know Jack's a lovely boy, that's not going to change.

FREYA. No it might. In certain ways. That's why he has to be assessed.

COLETTE. Freya, this isn't one of those occasions where you get to educate us all. We've had about enough of that.

FREYA. Enough of what?

COLETTE. You lecturing us on how we're meant to speak, what we're meant to think. We're not about to have a referendum on Jack. (*Changing the subject.*) Who makes eye contact with me all the time by the way. And he's noticed you being down lately too. Sure what did he say when he came in earlier? 'Auntie Freya is sad. That's why she's in pyjamas on my birthday.' I mean, so perceptive. There's no way that child is autistic.

ACT ONE   33

Pause. It's the first time the word's been said and it lands heavily in the room.

FREYA. Thanks, Mam.

COLETTE. I'm sorry, Helen, I – ...

SONYA. It's a spectrum.

Beat. SONYA *has the attention of the whole family.*

I don't know really, but I think it means there's lots of different types of...

HELEN. Exactly. It's not as easy as saying Jack understands emotions so he's fine. It's not how it works, apparently. If he is having difficulties we need to know so we can figure out what's best for him.

FREYA. Whatever you need, Hels, we'll do everything we can to support you. Sonya and I.

SONYA (*surprised to be included*). Definitely.

HELEN. Thanks.

COLETTE. And so will we, won't we, Tony?

TONY. Goes without saying.

COLETTE. Yes. But we're saying it.

TONY. Oh yeah, of course.

HELEN. I wanted you to know. That's all.

And Dad, I don't want you to feel bad about what happened, it's not your fault.

TONY. Thanks, Helen.

COLETTE. He got a bit of a shock when Tony roughhoused with him.

HELEN. Maybe.

COLETTE. Anyway, we'll wait for a proper... [diagnosis] result, because all this might be completely premature. We don't know anything yet.

HELEN. No. We don't.

COLETTE. Jack got a fright and there was nothing wrong with his reaction. Totally normal for a child of four.

HELEN. Anyway...

Beat.

FREYA. We better get going. We have a cat to find.

SONYA. Thanks, Colette... for the cake.

COLETTE. Oh well I'm sorry about that awful cake.

TONY (*to* SONYA). And I hope you get lucky.

(*Everyone's confused.*) With the cat!

SONYA. Oh right.

FREYA. You know, Dad, I'd side with my nephew over what happened earlier.

TONY. There's a surprise.

FREYA. Being touched when you least expect it – ugh! – Makes your skin crawl. You know? Everything heats up, you can't think and... I just want to break things.

Anyone would react badly to something like that.

TONY. Oh sure.

FREYA. Especially if you're four.

Beat.

SONYA (*awkward*). Shall we?

FREYA. It's like Jack sending himself to bed with his bedtime stories. (*To* SONYA.) When we were small, Helen always wanted to stay up late. She'd be quiet watching telly, hoping Mam and Dad wouldn't notice and I'd announce, 'It's past our bedtime.' Do you remember, Hels? You'd be raging.

HELEN. I remember.

FREYA. Now it's Jack sending himself to bed. The dote.

A very pregnant pause.

HELEN. Bye, Sonya.

SONYA (*distracted*). Yeah, great to see you, Helen.

HELEN. You too.

FREYA. We'll hit the road.

SONYA *doesn't move*.

Sonya?

SONYA. I just... I'm wondering if... ehm, Helen?

HELEN *offers her attention reluctantly*.

Do you think Freya could be... in some way... like Jack?

FREYA. What?

Beat.

HELEN. What do you mean, Sonya?

SONYA. Whatever Jack is... I'm wondering if you think that could be a possibility, for Freya?

FREYA. Sonya?

COLETTE (*flustered*). Jack isn't anything.

Why would you say something like that?

SONYA. It's probably nothing. But it occurred to me –

FREYA. That I might be...?

SONYA *looks at* FREYA.

That's... ridiculous.

COLETTE. Yes!

FREYA. I've hardly got this far, Sonya... without...

There's no way.

SONYA. Sure. Sorry. I don't know why I said it.

FREYA. That's hilarious, Son. I don't like to be touched so that makes me...

I know I get overwhelmed, but –

COLETTE. We can all get overwhelmed.

FREYA. Exactly!

Beat.

But I do see what Sonya's getting at.

You're always saying I overreact to everything.

COLETTE. But this is completely different.

SONYA. Is it, though?

HELEN. Sonya!? We don't know what this is.

SONYA. Of course.

I'm sorry.

FREYA (*to* SONYA). You madser!

Another beat.

We should go.

FREYA *doesn't move.*

Lots of kids prefer to be on their own… don't they? Not having friends hardly says – … I had nothing in common with kids my age. I'd get obsessed with things – like those farm animals – and nobody else cared as much but, that doesn't mean anything.

COLETTE. Of course it doesn't.

TONY. Look, it's your sister we should be worrying about right now. And Jack.

COLETTE. Exactly.

FREYA. Unless you think I could be… [on the spectrum.] Could have been all this time.

Well, do you?

Helen?

Sonya?

SONYA. Do you think you could be?

ACT ONE   37

FREYA. I don't know. What does that even...? Helen, what would that mean?

HELEN. I can't have this conversation with you, Freya.

FREYA. Why not?

HELEN. Take a wild guess.

Beat.

FREYA. I know, I'm sorry.

HELEN. My god. I'm just a little worn out worrying about my four-year-old child right now to be thinking how all this might reflect on you, my adult sister.

FREYA. It's only –

HELEN. Your narcissism knows / no bounds.

FREYA. Narcissism?

TONY. Girls!

HELEN. Whatever Sonya says, this is not about you, Freya! Do you hear me? It's about Jack.

FREYA. I know it's about Jack. Of course it's about Jack.

But what if I'm / on a... –

HELEN. Really?

FREYA. All my life I've struggled with... life.

I have drive. Don't I have drive, Sonya? You always said you wished you had my – And then you didn't because you said I was too much. I had too much drive. No one can keep up with me, that's what you said.

COLETTE. What are you saying?

FREYA. Is my 'drive', obsessive interests? Is that what that is?

TONY. Really, Freya. Sonya. We can't have this conversation now. None of us can.

FREYA. Sure. Of course.

SONYA. I'm sorry.

TONY. Helen, I'll drop you home.

TONY goes for his jacket and car keys.

FREYA. I'll stop. I've stopped now.

COLETTE. I'm going upstairs. I'll call you later, Helen. Goodbye, Sonya.

HELEN rises as TONY has his jacket on.

FREYA (*as* HELEN *passes*). I'm sorry, Helen, really I'm –

SONYA. Bye, Colette.

TONY (*to* FREYA). Your sister is upset so… not another word.

TONY and HELEN are gone.

COLETTE (*to* SONYA). It was… lovely seeing you again.

COLETTE exits. Pause.

SONYA. I shouldn't have said anything.

What do I know?… You know?

FREYA. I never stopped those kids from playing with the farm animals. They refused to come near me. I was always, weird, growing up. Talked too much. Like some alien. I talked too much but somehow, always about the wrong things. You would think some time I had to get it right. No one ever listened. Until you.

SONYA. I don't remember that.

FREYA. Maybe this is why.

You had so much trouble with me, Sonya. This could be why.

I thought it was because I was queer. I thought it was because I was a feminist. But what if? I'm not difficult, I'm… undiagnosed? And my whole family missed it all these years?!

SONYA. You really think – ?

FREYA. I don't know. I need to find out. How do I find out?

SONYA. But it feels like…?

FREYA. What? What should it feel like?

SONYA. It makes a kind of sense to you?

FREYA. Does it make sense to you?

I've always been... different. How do you know when different is...

I don't know how it feels to be another way.

SONYA. Poor Jack.

FREYA *absorbs this*.

FREYA. At least there might be a pair of us in it. I'll look out for him.

Beat.

SONYA. I didn't know, you weren't going to the office.

FREYA. I wore my repeal jumper in for dress-down Friday.

SONYA. What's wrong with that?

FREYA. Nothing. Except someone made a comment. Ava, Ava made a comment. Like how the battle was won already and we should all move on. That kind of horseshit.

SONYA. Wow.

FREYA. Yeah, exactly. But it was crazy, Sonya, I started crying. Right there. In front of everyone.

SONYA. You never cry.

FREYA. I know, I never do that but I... couldn't stop. I'm a trainee solicitor, standing in the middle of an open-plan office, and I'm sobbing.

And I was probably crying for us, you know, because we had just happened and Mary Robinson was gone and that was, a lot. Or maybe because stupidity like Ava's still exists in the world, who can tell? But I had to go home cos it was like, half-eleven in the morning and it was a whole thing and I couldn't stop crying so. HR got in touch. I'm taking some time.

Beat.

I'll go get my things.

SONYA. What?

FREYA. To come with you. I won't be long.

SONYA. To look for Mary Robinson?

FREYA. Yeah. We'll fly around Harold's Cross and then we'll go home. Just the two of us.

You want me to come home with you, right?

SONYA. But –

FREYA. But what?

SONYA. This doesn't really change anything? Between you and me. It doesn't change what happened.

FREYA. Not literally, no. It wasn't going well for a while –

SONYA. For a long while.

FREYA. ...And you ended it, sent me packing. Gave me the old heave-ho.

SONYA. I made a stand.

FREYA. And that made sense at the time. But now there's... new evidence. A new character witness.

SONYA. We don't know for sure.

FREYA. We know you see me, Sonya.

SONYA. It could explain things. Things about us.

FREYA. You thought I wasn't trying. You thought I wouldn't change. But what if... What if I was trying all this time. Maybe that's all it was.

SONYA. Maybe.

FREYA. And I've been trying since then too.

SONYA. You stopped talking to me. You stopped taking my calls.

FREYA. You knew where I was. It's not like I disappeared.

And now you're here.

SONYA. I don't know if this is a good idea. I mean, I'm doing well. I think I'm doing well.

FREYA *smirks*.

FREYA (*gently*). We're about to trawl suburbia on the suggestion of a loony octogenarian. It's hardly peak mental health.

You called over for a reason.

SONYA. Okay, yes! Maybe I did, but… you have a lot to figure out.

FREYA. We have a lot to figure out. We can do it together. Son, Sonya. Lovely Sonya.

This could be a whole new start for us. A whole new life. I promise.

FREYA *and* SONYA *look at each other.*

Lights out.

ACT TWO

Music plays. The cast playfully rearrange the set to assemble:

The kitchen cum living room of Sonya's flat. A sense of them enjoying playing house again. The bedroom is off the main space as is a corridor/hall leading to the front door, off. There's a bonsai tree. The flat's not on the ground floor and there's a buzzer system.

Music/lights fade...

FREYA *is on the couch lit up by the glow of a laptop. Tears stream down her face as she scrolls. We sense she's been crying for a long time. She hears something, looks over her shoulder, then moves into the bedroom hurriedly.*

SONYA *enters on her mobile. We hear her before we see her.*

SONYA. No, you're very good to call, thanks, Loretta. Just next time, if you could manage to get a picture first, then we'd know.

Beat. SONYA *drops her bag, taking in the flat approvingly; maybe she strokes a blanket of Freya's that's lying where she was sitting.*

See for myself? Wait, Loretta, is Mary Robinson there now?

FREYA (*off, from the bedroom*). You should read these testimonies.

SONYA (*to* FREYA, *covering the phone*). Yeah hi, I'm home.

FREYA. Maddening!

SONYA (*back to Loretta with a lowered voice*). So you can take the picture. You can take a picture of her now.

Beat.

Right. Call me back after. Thanks...

SONYA *hangs up just as* FREYA *enters, laptop in hand.*

...Hi! Everything okay?

FREYA. We need more wardrobe space. Were you talking to someone?

SONYA. You're not dressed.

FREYA. It's like your stuff expanded while I was away. Did we go in for some retail therapy?

SONYA (*sarcastic*). With all my spare cash.

FREYA. I could have sworn I had the whole right-hand side. Did I not have the right-hand side?

Of the wardrobe.

SONYA. I don't know.

FREYA. It's hard to play the domestic goddess when there isn't a place for everything. I watched a bunch of home-organiser vids this morning and they're very big on having a place for everything. That and see-through boxes. They love a transparent box.

SONYA. Don't we all? Sorry... [for the weird joke.]

You don't have to play domestic goddess.

FREYA. Who was on the phone?

SONYA. Just... Loretta. (*Pre-empting.*) Guess what? She's in her back garden right now. She's been lying there for half an hour.

FREYA. Mary Robinson? (*Patronisingly.*) Sonya.

SONYA. I know the probability is –

FREYA *moves to the couch.*

FREYA. Nil. (*French.*) Nul points.

SONYA. I know that but... she's getting a photograph. So we can be certain. Either way.

FREYA *sits down, reading her laptop.*

FREYA. I'll need more of the wardrobe.

SONYA. Thanks for tidying up.

FREYA. The benefits of having a kept woman.

SONYA. Hardly.

FREYA. And I watered that bonsai. What you were thinking getting one of those?

SONYA. I had an impulse.

FREYA. They're so temperamental. Why take that on?

SONYA. I can sustain things.

FREYA. Oh I know. You've got stickability. (*Pushing away her laptop.*) So, tell me about your day. Susan still loving your work?

SONYA. She called my reports 'insightful'... Go, me! Don't know why I stressed so much.

FREYA. Because you care. That's a good thing.

SONYA. I suppose.

FREYA. There is such a thing as healthy stress.

SONYA. I'm not sure I'm there yet.

FREYA. Tell me about it.

Beat. SONYA *checks her phone.*

Y'know, having this space to look at myself, this time?... It's helping, Sonya.

SONYA. Did you speak to your family today?

FREYA. They're not cross with you.

SONYA. It's not that, it's... Haven't they been trying to contact you?

FREYA. I'm not talking to them.

SONYA. Like, ever?

FREYA. Je refuse.

SONYA. But I thought –

Sonya's mobile rings.

FREYA. Loola calling!

SONYA (*answering*). Loretta, yes? How did you get on? (*Beat. Disappointed.*) Oh. Oh that's a pity. (*Beat. Quietly.*) But why did you – ? You could see her from the window. So why go outside?

FREYA. Because she's doolally.

SONYA. Well if she comes back, please only contact me after. Can you do that for me?

FREYA. Sonya!

SONYA *makes an appealing gesture to* FREYA.

SONYA (*to Loretta and* FREYA). I know, I know.

You're very good, Loretta, I appreciate it.

Beat.

But isn't he in Australia? Oh if he was there, he'd have been able to – yeah, I understand. I see what you mean, Loretta. Every morning? (*Pretending to be impressed.*) Well!

(*Turning away from* FREYA, *with real intimacy.*) …Yes. She is a beautiful cat. We do miss her.

FREYA *surprisingly takes* SONYA*'s hand to support her. They make eye contact.*

We miss her, every day. Thanks, Loretta. I know. Bye. Bye bye.

SONYA *hangs up, exhausted.*

FREYA. You're a glutton for punishment.

SONYA. I know. I know I am. I told her to take the photo and only then – But she's a little –

FREYA. Yes, she is.

SONYA. She's on her own. Her only son's emigrated and I think she likes having someone – [to talk to.]

FREYA. Which would be fine if you weren't an emotional wreck by the end of every phone call. You're like her personal agony aunt at this stage.

SONYA (*defiant*). I'm fine.

FREYA. Really?

SONYA. I'm not the one in pyjamas at six o'clock in the evening. Please get dressed.

FREYA. Are we going out?

SONYA. It's good for your... you know, sense of self. Starting the day. It's one of the things I learned in our... time to ourselves. The importance of making yourself presentable. Ready to face the world.

FREYA. At six o'clock in the evening?

SONYA. You feel better for it.

FREYA (*signalling her laptop*). You should read these threads, Sonya. All these women who go undiagnosed. A lot of them way older than me. And you know why? Gender bias in the medical profession. Women present in such a different way to men they're only starting to notice now, in the freakin' twenty-first century.

(*Off* SONYA*'s look.*) But you know what? I'm not going to rage. I'm going to disconnect emotionally. Ironic, cos that's like a superpower for lots of these women. But you know what they say, if you've met one person with ASD, you've met one person with –

SONYA. Won't you get dressed?

FREYA. If you really want me to.

SONYA. I do.

FREYA (*playfully*). You'll only be taking them back off me in an hour or so. Thought you liked me in my PJs. Find them sexy.

SONYA. You've a stain.

FREYA. Ugh. That was lunch.

SONYA. Can I have the laptop? There's a work email I have to – [write.]

ACT TWO   47

FREYA. Hang on.

> FREYA *gives* SONYA *a passionate kiss*.

Last night…

> SONYA *giggles*.

Why weren't we always – [like that?]

SONYA. What you mean? We were!

FREYA. It was great.

SONYA (*delighted*). Yeah. I wanted to again this morning.

FREYA. Why didn't you?

SONYA. Oh, I don't know. You looked peaceful. Lying there.

FREYA. Disturb the peace.

SONYA. What?

FREYA. Disturb the peace, Sonya. Make a disturbance. You can wake me for that, any time.

> *They kiss again.*

SONYA. Love you.

FREYA. Love you.

> *Beat.*

SONYA. It has been good.

FREYA. Being back?

SONYA. Seeing you peaceful. It's new.

FREYA. Peaceful? I'm not sure I'm there yet.

I'll get rid of this [top], shall I?

SONYA. Please.

> SONYA *starts writing her email on the laptop, while* FREYA *changes*.

FREYA. And on top of bias in the medical profession, you've also got media bias.

SONYA. Wow, you've got a lot of tabs open here.

FREYA. Tell me about it.

> Now I'm not going to rage but... *Rain Man*. When did that come out, the eighties? That's an extreme example, but there's been so many. Yet we're still waiting to see a female-presenting neurodiverse character on anything. Anything mainstream at least. Or maybe there is and I don't know about it, but if so, why?

SONYA *mouths along with the first two words:*

> Gender bias in the media. So we're twice damned. (I saw that.) We need to be able to see every type, every type of person. We need to see it all. Oh my god, Sonya! We need transparent boxes.

> You have to read the testimonies of these women. It's like Alice stepping through the looking glass for most of them. Or like, the opposite. They've been in this strange wonderland and suddenly everything's explained for them. Suddenly it all makes sense.

SONYA. And is that how you're feeling?

FREYA. Well I've got you. So it's hard to separate. How's this?

SONYA. You look great.

FREYA. Thank you.

A quick kiss.

SONYA. Let me just...

A pause while SONYA *composes her email and* FREYA *waits with little to do.*

FREYA. I need more wardrobe. My things won't fit.

SONYA (*under breath, still typing*). Sure.

FREYA. I have been going over... [everything.]

> What we argued about. Why we... took some time.

SONYA. Can I finish...?

FREYA. Not to rehearse old arguments, but I can't help thinking, was that me? Was it my fault? Or was it the result of... you know.

SONYA. Send. (*Giving her full attention.*) But we don't know yet / if you are – [on the spectrum.]

FREYA. I'm starting to suspect... things.

SONYA. That's news.

FREYA. There's online tests.

SONYA. They're not comprehensive, / you said.

FREYA. And I think what happened with us – our communication problems – the way I see it now, it's like what's going on all around us, in a much bigger macro way.

SONYA. You've lost me.

FREYA. Well, take your singing for example.

SONYA. My – ?

FREYA. When I asked you to stop singing in the flat. I said it had nothing to do with you being a bad singer. But you didn't believe me. Your feelings were hurt.

SONYA. We never argued over that.

FREYA. You sulked. You sulked a bit.

SONYA. Oh really.

FREYA. I'm saying it's probably got more to do with sensory overload.

I mean, I wondered about that myself. If I like your singing voice – which I do, Sonya, I think you have a lovely singing voice. So why does it do my head in listening to you warbling every hour of the day?

SONYA. Warbling?

FREYA. I didn't like asking you not to sing, Sonya. And I know you don't believe me. You think I'm deliberately being hurtful and that couldn't be further from the truth.

SONYA. I never said that.

FREYA. I'm only giving it as an example.

SONYA. But why?

FREYA. As an illustration. Or a thought experiment. If you can see something like this – an example of me being, 'controlling' or whatever – if you can flip that around and think, 'wow, she was able to put up with my singing for so long, even though it caused her physical pain.'

SONYA. Right.

FREYA. No, it's like that, Sonya. It's physically painful for us.

SONYA. Us?

FREYA. The neuroatypical community. It can cause us actual pain.

It's like as if I was sunburned, okay? Imagine you can actually see my sunburn. And you're wearing a top made out of sandpaper.

SONYA. What?

FREYA. The outside is sandpaper. Not the inside. The inside is satin.

SONYA. But why would anyone –

FREYA. Just imagine it for a second. You can visualise how painful a hug would be, right? I'm sunburnt and you're wearing a sandpaper top and you're rubbing, as in moving up and down on me, think of how painful that is.

I should cry out, shouldn't I? I should scream 'Get away from me.' But I don't. To save your feelings, I don't. I say, 'Sonya, I love that you're a loving person but... – '

SONYA. Okay – I don't want to... [get into this –] I get your point.

FREYA. Really?

SONYA. I cause you pain, and you're the patient one because you don't cry out.

ACT TWO   51

FREYA. Yes!

SONYA. So if I could see everything from that point of view, I'd know that really you're amazing and the problem is entirely mine to deal with.

FREYA. Kind of, but –

SONYA. So I should be the one changing and adapting.

FREYA. No, I'm on a journey with this too.

SONYA. But essentially, it's all my fault.

FREYA. No!

SONYA. It's entirely my fault.

FREYA. I'm not trying to place blame here.

SONYA. Well I feel blamed.

FREYA. And that's the problem, Sonya.

SONYA. Oh I've a problem now?

FREYA. No it's the problem. I haven't tried to blame you for anything. But immediately you take it on yourself. That wasn't my point actually, placing blame wasn't at all my point. Yet you feel attacked.

SONYA. Well forgive me for not being able to see your sunburn while I'm chafing you!

FREYA. It's a metaphor.

SONYA. I thought your community wasn't supposed to be good with those.

FREYA. Don't take the piss. And again, that's a very male form of presenting you're describing there. Women are usually way better with language, and masking in general.

SONYA. Masking?

FREYA. It's how we learn to get by. To hide our difficulties.

SONYA. Look, can we not right now?

FREYA. What?

SONYA. Start analysing our entire relationship.

FREYA. But I'm not talking about us. Well, I am. But I'm also talking about society in general. And how hard it is for those of us who experience real difference to make our case without causing offence. I think it's a profound point.

SONYA. Look, I know you've been home on your own all day, so you've got plenty you want to, offload, but can we… I don't know… figure out dinner and maybe after…

FREYA. I'm only saying in this case, you represent the dominant in society. Yet look how impossible it is to talk about certain things without upsetting you. The dominant group becomes so touchy when asked to make even the smallest allowance for those who are different. Because heaven forbid we offend anyone, or make you feel even mildly uncomfortable. Yet we're the flakes. Do you see what I mean?

Beat.

SONYA. So in this scenario, I am… dominant?

FREYA. What?

SONYA. I represent the dominant in society. I dominate.

FREYA *looks at* SONYA, *confused*.

So what you're saying is… I'm in charge?

FREYA. What's going on?

SONYA. According to you, whatever I say goes, and you will submit. Because I am dominant.

FREYA (*getting the game*). If you want to be.

SONYA. I want to be.

FREYA. You can be dominant.

SONYA. I can be *so* dominant.

FREYA. You can be the fucking patriarchy.

SONYA. Sexy. Not really, but you know what I mean – I like being dominant.

ACT TWO   53

FREYA. What are you going to do, Sonya, with all that power?

SONYA. After I solve the climate crisis and create a more equitable society?

FREYA. Obvs.

SONYA. I don't know, I don't know. Maybe I'll order you – into that bedroom and –

The intercom alert goes – BUZZ. Beat.

Oh shit.

FREYA. Who's that?

SONYA. Why don't you answer?

FREYA. Who's it going to be?

BUZZ. FREYA answers.

Hello?

HELEN (*via the intercom*). Hi, it's me.

FREYA. Helen?

HELEN. Yeah, look. Can I come up?

FREYA. No, I'm not... We're not... Nope.

FREYA hangs up.

SONYA. Freya!

FREYA (*to* SONYA). You knew.

SONYA. She rang me this afternoon. I said she could call round.

(*On the intercom, buzzing her through.*) Hi Helen, come on up.

HELEN (*on the intercom*). Thanks, Sonya.

FREYA. Why didn't you ask me?

SONYA. Because I knew you'd say no. Look, you can't cut ties with your entire family. We can't – we need them. We need at least half a proper family.

FREYA. Why?

A knock on the door.

SONYA. Talk to her. See what she has to say.

> FREYA *goes to answer.* SONYA *puts the laptop away.* FREYA *traipses back in,* HELEN *in tow.*

Hi Helen.

HELEN. Hi. Hi Freya.

> FREYA *gives a half-hearted wave.*

How are you both doing?

SONYA. We're great. I'm still in work clothes actually… I'll change quickly. Do you want something? Freya will look after you. Frey?

> SONYA *exits into the bedroom. Beat.*

HELEN. So things are working out for you two?

FREYA. Things are great.

HELEN. Ah that's brilliant. I'm delighted for you.

FREYA *(slightly hushed)*. They're sort of great.

HELEN. Oh. Still ironing out the creases?

FREYA. No, there's no creases. Sonya's amazing and I'm – …

HELEN. Over the moon to have her back?

Beat.

FREYA. Yeah, absolutely. Couldn't be happier.

Beat.

What you want then?

HELEN. Sorry?

FREYA. Why have you come? To the flat?

HELEN. Oh… welcoming… Okay then…

> Jack saw the specialist yesterday. We still don't know anything. He's going to have a few appointments and well,

while I was in there, I made some enquiries. Y'know, for adults. For someone an adult might see. So... Here. It's the details of a psychologist you could call.

HELEN *offers a page with information on it*. FREYA *accepts*.

You do two interviews apparently. One with a psychologist and another with a SALT, em –

FREYA. A Speech and Language / Therapist –

HELEN. Therapist, yeah. I think. Maybe that's only for Jack, I'm not sure – but there's a second opinion involved.

FREYA. And they ask your family to fill out a questionnaire about your childhood.

HELEN. That's right. Have you seen someone?

FREYA. Read up online. (*Re: the information, graciously.*) Thanks.

HELEN. I'm still not sure, you know. Gary took Jack swimming on the weekend and I was worried. I mean, we were all worried because swimming pools on a Saturday morning? – they're loud, full of people, splashing about – potential nightmare for Jack. But he loved it! Yeah. Loved his little armbands, kicking his legs. Started chatting to the other kids, spontaneously, off his own bat. And there were giggles, hollering – no fear. Don't think the specialist found much wrong with Jack either.

What that means for you...

Either way. I'm sorry I got angry. At Mam and Dad's. I was processing myself and I wasn't in a place, to deal.

Beat.

FREYA. You're never in a place.

HELEN. What does that mean?

FREYA. You never had any time for me.

HELEN. You think that?

FREYA. I'd follow you around. Everywhere. You were always trying to get rid of me.

HELEN. You drove me nuts. From a young age. Yes.

FREYA. If I'd been in a wheelchair –

HELEN. What?

FREYA. A simple thought experiment. If I'd been in a wheelchair, do you think you would have been so quick to run away? Lock your door? Do you think Mam and Dad would have let you?

HELEN. I only got a door age twelve. You had your own room from seven. Think about that.

FREYA. I didn't want my own room. I needed you.

HELEN. You weren't disabled. Is that what you're getting at with the wheelchair?

FREYA. I needed help with things. When did you ever help me?

HELEN. Well I tried to with boys. I wasn't to know, was I? And with clothes, make-up.

FREYA. You never helped with anything important.

Beat.

HELEN. Sarcasm. I taught you sarcasm, remember? 'I really love peas, Mammy, thanks so much for putting them on my plate!' Was that something important?

FREYA *nods, smiling*.

'Oh my god, Dad, you look awesome in those chinos. And you're right, Leonard Cohen is a genius!'

They laugh. FREYA *stops*.

FREYA. Do you think sarcasm is something you should have to be taught?

HELEN. Sorry?

FREYA. Is it not something you should, know?

HELEN. Maybe.

Beat.

And long division.

FREYA. What?

HELEN. I taught you long division. Two years early. So there's two things. Sarcasm and long division.

FREYA. Oh well, great! I hate maths. And that's not unusual, despite prevailing narratives.

HELEN. What are you on about?

SONYA *enters in softer clothes*.

SONYA. I'm having a glass of wine. Helen?

HELEN. I will, thanks.

SONYA. Freya?

FREYA. Not for me. Midweek and all.

SONYA. I find it helps to unwind. Stress of the day. Here you go.

HELEN. Thanks. So you're not at that coffee place any more?

SONYA. My barista days are behind me, sadly. After Freya... [moved out] I needed to make proper money to cover rent so...

FREYA. I would have helped you.

SONYA. I didn't want help. One of the regulars –

FREYA. Susan!

SONYA. Yes, Susan. Susan works for iCharity and there was an admin job going. Full time. Turns out to be way more responsibility than I was expecting. But I'm coping.

FREYA. Susan has a gift for spotting talent apparently.

HELEN. Does she now?

FREYA. That's what she told me.

SONYA. Freya joined the Friday drinks.

FREYA. She's spotted something, that Susan, that's all I'll say.

HELEN. Freya, are you jealous?

SONYA. She's like fifteen years older than me. 'Sake.

FREYA. But she looks great. Swims in the sea every morning. Said we should join her. Like, could she be more cliché? Probably will though.

SONYA (*to* HELEN). I thought Freya would be happy for me.

FREYA. I am happy for you.

SONYA. She's always saying I need to… expand, or whatever. Take my place in the world. And it's for a good cause. It has meaning, you know?

FREYA. It's a great job. They all love her, as they should.

HELEN. What's the charity?

SONYA. Well it's a tech company makes it easier for people to donate. So in a way, all of them.

HELEN. Oh right.

SONYA. But it's a not-for-profit.

HELEN. That's great, Sonya. Congrats.

SONYA. Cheers.

FREYA (*pouring herself a glass*). Yeah, cheers. To new life experiences. And to Susan. Chin-chin.

Beat.

HELEN. You'll make that appointment.

FREYA. I suppose I'll have to. No one is going to do it for me.

HELEN. You know Mam and Dad are properly bothered. Mam's seething. You could have told her you were moving out. She's taking it personally.

FREYA. Oh for her it's personal? Spare me.

HELEN. I hope she does! Honestly, Colette is losing it. Like with Jack. She keeps insisting he's fine. Pointing out his tiniest achievements. 'Oh look, Jack ate all his sandwiches, even the crusts!' She's getting on with Gary now too which is, strange. She got him to tell her the swimming pool story like, three times. (*To* SONYA.) Jack loved the swimming pool. (*Back to* FREYA.) I swear it's all she wants to talk about. The woman needs help, Frey. Give her a call, will you?

Beat. FREYA *sips her wine.*

SONYA. How is Jack doing?

HELEN. Loved his first appointment. Lots of attention and the specialist lets him play. He was in great form. It could all turn out to be nothing.

SONYA. Oh.

HELEN. No one will confirm anything which is – (*Sarcastic.*) just a teeny bit stressful… and supports keep getting mentioned, supports are available. And I do this myself as a claims adjustor: playing out multiple scenarios, talking to clients, committing to absolutely nothing until there's a full evaluation. So you would think I'd be okay with a period of uncertainty but… It's the not knowing at this stage that's… (*She mimes her head exploding.*)

SONYA. Right. That's tough.

FREYA. It shouldn't have to be.

Whatever happens, there's no reason why this should hinder any aspect of Jack's life.

HELEN. You think?

FREYA. If society's awareness grows. Lots of humanity's greatest breakthroughs are down to neurodiverse thinking. Really, it's a gift.

SONYA. Seriously?

FREYA. That's rude, Sonya.

SONYA. Oh. (*To* HELEN.) Sorry, I didn't mean –

HELEN. Don't worry.

SONYA (*to* FREYA). But you're calling it a gift now?

FREYA. It can be. If society recognised the effort people put into masking their supposed difficulties. If we didn't have to spend our time doing that but could put our energies into following our unique paths, without fears of not fitting in or getting bullied and brutalised. Promise me, Helen, promise you won't treat Jack like he has a disability. You won't make him feel like he's any less, just because he's different.

HELEN. Sure. Of course, but…

FREYA. But what?

HELEN. What about that whole wheelchair analogy? Now you don't want to be treated like you're different?

FREYA. I want our difference to be celebrated.

HELEN (*wry*). Oh well, yes. Of course you do.

FREYA. What's that supposed to mean?

HELEN. Oh nothing.

FREYA. No, go on.

HELEN. I don't want to argue.

FREYA. Then don't.

HELEN. Okay then.

Beat.

FREYA. But say what you're thinking. Not this passive-aggressive 'of course you do'. What's wrong with wanting to be celebrated? Society could do with a little more empathy. It's sorely lacking in the world.

HELEN. When I came in here, Sonya, Freya accused me of never having any time for her. Can you believe that? I mean, you were there for almost half of it so you can say. Did Freya get no attention from me? Or more truthfully, was it not the case that every hour of every day, every family meal, every holiday and celebration, we spent our entire time talking about Freya's problems, Freya's campaigns, her every neuroses. I couldn't breathe without my little sister deflecting towards whatever was going on in her life. Because she was queer. And feminist – which I was first by the way – and so alternative and everything else under the sun, my petty boy problems never got a look-in. Nor my studies. When I had to repeat, you slagged me mercilessly. I got engaged to Gary and I knew you were disappointed in me. Like I betrayed the sisterhood by getting pregnant. Even when Mam had her scare, it became all about you. The test comes back benign but we still have to deal with your existential angst, Sonya knows all about it.

FREYA. I don't understand how you could all be so relaxed about it. I still don't.

HELEN. About death?! We're not. No one is! We just don't have to advertise and analyse and be consumed by our every inner thought and emotion.

FREYA. But that's probably my Asperger's! That's what I mean. Society has to learn how to deal with magical thinking.

HELEN. Magical thinking?! From the moment you could talk, I got usurped in my own home. By a teeny-tiny tyrant. From the moment you could talk, I was never allowed breath without first having to check what the effect was going to be on you. I lost everything. Independence, a place of my own, space for my own feelings. And it was draining!

FREYA (*sarcastic*). Poor Hels!

Beat. HELEN *can't help smirking.*

HELEN. It's not like you were an entertaining sort of needy either. Until you hit puberty. It wasn't until you came out it became any sort of fun! At least there was that. You know, I think I only started to like you about ten years ago.

FREYA. Oh well, great.

HELEN. I do like you, Freya. Never a dull moment and all that. I mean, who else comes out to their parents by having sex in their spare room?

FREYA. We weren't having sex!

HELEN. Whatever you were doing.

SONYA. Poor Tony!

HELEN. Yeah god, poor Dad. Got the shock of his life that night. Imagine walking in on that! And I remember they were both so excited you were having your first sleepover instead of ruining mine like you always did. I think it was his giddiness actually made him check up on you.

FREYA. It was past midnight. I thought the coast was clear.

SONYA. It was my second shock that night. When Freya crept in my bed, I had no idea what was going on.

FREYA. Neither did I.

They hold hands.

SONYA. We had never talked about it. I never even told her I was gay.

HELEN. It was pretty obvious.

SONYA. To the rest of the world maybe.

HELEN. I'm glad you're back together. Going to separate colleges – that's hard on any relationship.

SONYA. My dropping out didn't help either.

FREYA. Wasn't the right fit.

SONYA. Some people thrive in university…

FREYA. You could have. You were on the wrong course.

SONYA. You thrived. You joined every committee going.

FREYA. I have 'drive'.

SONYA. I always had Freya to sort of… I mean, she was so sure of everything. She called out homophobia on the corridors, she would bawl the lads out of it and didn't care.

I could never.

But college… I felt young there, or. Couldn't talk to people. I didn't have, words.

HELEN. Not something we Pattisons ever suffered from.

SONYA. And then we were on separate tracks.

FREYA. Jesus. You make it sound like such a struggle.

SONYA. Well it was there for a time. I think you get so used to struggling, after a while, you don't notice it any more.

FREYA. Sonya?

HELEN. That sounds difficult.

FREYA (*finding the sympathy patronising*). Yeah, Helen, thanks.

HELEN. What?

Beat.

FREYA. Tell you what. Tony got what he deserved that night. Do you remember?

HELEN. He was mortified.

SONYA. He was mortified?!

FREYA. You know I'm still not sure how Dad voted. On the big one. Bet he went the other way. Can you believe that? He still goes to Mass. Even Mam has given that up.

HELEN. He's allowed go to Mass, Freya. He's gone his whole life. We're talking about a car dealer who married a trolley dolly, yet somehow managed to raise the pair of us.

FREYA. Dragged more like.

HELEN. She thought he was a rock star when he rolled up in one of those vintage cars. And he found her uniform the height of eighties glam. Is it any wonder our family struggles with reality?

FREYA *sniggers*.

What?

FREYA. I just got the irony. All his restoring of cars and she's the one who married a fixer-upper!

HELEN. It's not funny. We're lucky they survived. I thought one of those votes would break our family. Serious. You were so bound up in them. You both were.

FREYA. Well it was only the validity of our love – and then our bodies! – that was at stake. Sorry if a decade of arguing for our right to exist was stressful for you.

HELEN. For everyone.

FREYA. It wasn't your life being debated.

HELEN. A point you made countless times at the dinner table. And they listened, didn't they? Not at first but…

They've done all right, considering, Colette and Tony. Come a long way.

Beat.

Still, some way to find out your little girl isn't a little girl any more.

FREYA. She's into girls!

SONYA. Oh Jesus it was cringe.

But they were good about it. After they got used to the idea. Better than my mam, right? They've always been good to me, Freya. You should talk to them.

BUZZ. The intercom again. Beat. Everyone surprised.

FREYA. Do we know who this is?

SONYA *shakes her head*. FREYA *answers*.

Hello?

TONY (*via the intercom*). Freya?

FREYA. Speak of the fucking devil!

She buzzes him through, unthinking.

Did he hear us?

(*To* SONYA.) Did you know about this too?

SONYA (*holding up her hands*). [No.] Honestly.

FREYA (*to* HELEN). Did you?

HELEN. No idea.

FREYA. Well what does he want?

HELEN. To talk to you, I imagine.

FREYA. Is Mam with him?

HELEN. How should I know?

There's a knock on the door.

SONYA. Get the door.

FREYA. No. I won't be ambushed in my own place.

SONYA. Freya!

FREYA. I'm not answering.

Another knock.

SONYA. Let him in.

Beat.

HELEN. I'll go.

HELEN *goes out into the corridor.*

FREYA. I don't want to see him.

SONYA. I know nothing about this, I swear.

FREYA *escapes into the bedroom just before* HELEN *arrives back with* TONY.

TONY. Where's Freya?

SONYA. Bedroom.

Beat.

TONY. She doesn't want to see me? Can't say I blame her. With all she's going through.

HELEN. It's not your fault. It was a different time.

FREYA (*off*). What, the nineties?

HELEN (*raised voice so* FREYA *can hear*). There wasn't the same level of understanding.

Beat.

TONY (*wary*). How are you, Sonya?

SONYA. I'm fine, Tony. Having a glass of white. Would you like – [some?]

TONY. No, I'm all right. I wanted to give Freya this.

TONY *produces a sheaf of papers.*

I filled it out for her.

SONYA. What is it?

TONY. Oh a questionnaire thing. She emailed it to us.

FREYA (*entering*). I sent that to Mam.

TONY. That's right.

FREYA. But you filled it out? Or did you both do it?

TONY. What does it matter?

FREYA. Well, don't take this the wrong way, Dad, but I kind of trust Mam's opinion more than I do yours.

TONY. Oh. Right.

FREYA. Women are better at remembering detail, that's all.

TONY. Well I think I remember you as a toddler, Freya. You were fairly memorable.

(*To* SONYA, *gesturing to his forehead*.) Seared!

TONY *smirks at his quip. Beat.*

FREYA. I'm just a big joke to you, amn't I?

TONY. What? No! Not a bit.

FREYA. How can you make fun of my tantrums now?

TONY. No you're right, you're right. Fair enough. I didn't mean anything by it.

FREYA *starts to cry angry tears*.

Are you… crying?

FREYA. Uh-hunh. This is what I do now, apparently.

TONY (*tenderly*). Freya!

FREYA. How could you not see, Dad? How did you not…?

TONY. Oh Frey, I've been asking myself the same thing. Over and over. I've been thinking about nothing else for the last two weeks. How could we have missed it?

FREYA. Yeah.

TONY. And the truth is… we thought it was you, Freya. It was the way you were. So we rolled with it.

FREYA. Rolled with it?

TONY. Look, you did well in school. You were never in any danger. You got bullied a bit, I remember, but you could stand up for yourself. And you were happy, Freya. I remember you being very happy.

FREYA. You what?

(*To* HELEN.) Do you remember that?

Beat. The tears have stopped.

See, this is why I sent the questionnaire to Mam. No! No, I don't believe you. I was never happy. You got away with the bare minimum. Running to the garage whenever the oestrogen got too much for you. Letting Mam do all the heavy lifting. No!

You had time to notice. You had time to intervene. You didn't give a shit.

SONYA. Freya.

FREYA. It's true.

HELEN. Look, let's all calm down. We were just laughing, Dad, about the way Freya came out to you.

FREYA. And that's another thing!

Beat.

HELEN. What?

FREYA. It was past midnight. What were you doing checking up on us at that hour?

TONY. What's that?

FREYA. Sonya was staying in the spare room, do you remember? Because you thought we wouldn't sleep if we kept each other up all night, chatting in the same room.

HELEN. What are you talking about?

FREYA. Whatever about checking in on me. Why would you poke your nose into the spare room after midnight? To see if Sonya was all right? She's not your daughter. She was barely thirteen.

TONY. What are you saying?

SONYA. Freya?

FREYA. Explain it.

TONY. Explain what?

HELEN. Freya, what are you suggesting?

FREYA. I think we all know what I'm suggesting. You had no right to be coming into that room at that hour of the night. In all the commotion no one ever thought to ask, did they? But what the fuck were you doing going in there at that time?

HELEN. Jesus, Freya! You can't mean that.

FREYA. Explain it, Dad.

TONY. Explain what? What am I being accused of here?

FREYA. You know well what I'm accusing you of.

SONYA. Jesus Christ, Freya!

HELEN. You can't say that. Freya! Take it back immediately.

FREYA. Let's ask Mam, shall we?

TONY. What?

FREYA. Let's see what Mam makes of all of this.

HELEN. Freya!

FREYA *takes out her phone and speed-dials* COLETTE. *Everyone waits, slightly frozen and lost. Some theatricality here where* COLETTE *is visible either by projection or somewhere else on the stage.* COLETTE *rejects the call.*

FREYA. She declined the call. Hold on.

FREYA *dials again.*

HELEN. Freya, don't!

COLETTE *answers this time.* FREYA *puts her on speaker.*

COLETTE. What is it?

FREYA. Hi Mam, you doing anything?

COLETTE. Just watching the soaps.

FREYA. Right, hang on.

COLETTE. Hold on, I'm getting another call. Let me just –

ACT TWO   69

FREYA. No Mam, that's me. Jesus, she's as bad as Loretta.

COLETTE. There, I just had to get rid of that.

FREYA. No Mam, that's me. I'm trying to put you on video.

COLETTE. What? Oh there's another one, I better answer this in case it's something important.

FREYA. Something important? Charming.

COLETTE. Hello?

FREYA. Mam, Mammy –

COLETTE. Is that you, Freya?

FREYA. You're on video. Take the phone from your ear.

COLETTE. What? Oh. There you are.

FREYA. Hi Mam. I'm in our place. With Sonya. And Helen's here.

COLETTE. Oh right.

FREYA. And well, look who came for a visit.

FREYA points her camera at TONY.

TONY. Hi love.

COLETTE. Tony? What are you doing there?

FREYA (*to* TONY). I knew she didn't know you were calling. Hi Mam. Two things.

COLETTE. Yes, love?

FREYA. One, Dad's filled out that questionnaire I sent you. You didn't want him to do that, am I right?

Beat.

COLETTE. That's right.

FREYA. You weren't going to fill it out at all. Were you?

COLETTE. ... No, because it's completely ridiculous, Freya.

FREYA. Right, thanks, Mam. I suppose it's easier to deny everything rather than take the blame.

COLETTE. For what?

FREYA. For misunderstanding me my entire life.

COLETTE. Oh god. And what was the second thing?

FREYA. What?

COLETTE. You said there were two things.

FREYA. I'm not done with the first thing.

COLETTE. Well I am, Freya. I'm not about to enter into a discussion with you on this one.

FREYA. Fine!

FREYA *hangs up*.

That's enough from her. Jesus!

FREYA *collapses into the chair/couch*.

Pause.

TONY. What you just accused me of, Freya… is abhorrent. Utterly abhorrent. Are you going to apologise?

Pause.

FREYA. Bet you're in trouble now. Colette knows you caved. How soft, Dad.

HELEN. Shut up, Freya!

SONYA. I think you should both go now.

Beat.

Freya's not herself. It's a strange time for her and this isn't – [helping.] Helen? Will you take Mr Pattison with you?

Beat.

HELEN. Come on, Dad.

TONY. Freya, you can break things. You know that? You can't always fix them.

(*To* SONYA.) Goodnight, Sonya.

ACT TWO 71

HELEN *and* TONY *leave. Pause.*

FREYA. So much for peaceful.

Freya's phone pings. She looks at it.

The woman can't handle a video call but she manages to send voice notes.

SONYA. Colette?

FREYA. She hates texting. Let's hear what Mother has to say then, shall we?

FREYA *hits play on the voice message with her phone on speaker mode. Over the course of the message, the volume level amplifies to give a sense of how* FREYA *and* SONYA *are hearing it.*

COLETTE. Freya. When you moved home, do you know I was so worried about you? I spent three whole months doing nothing else, except worrying about you. How you'd cope without Sonya. How you'd get by. And we looked after you, Tony and I. We didn't pry. We didn't judge. We left you to grieve your relationship. Because we love you.

Well now you're throwing all that back in our faces. And your father's so good, he sneaked over to you tonight with that questionnaire all filled out. The fool. Well I'm no fool. You can have your sneaky appointments with your father. But I'm done. I'm done with you.

I love you, Freya. Do you hear me? I love you. But I don't like you.

Click! FREYA *and* SONYA *look at each other.*

Lights out.

Interval.

ACT THREE

Music plays. FREYA *and* SONYA *perform a dance number in shades with ice-cream cones.*

The set has already been reassembled:

A bench. There might be a fountain nearby. It's outside so any sense of clutter from earlier acts is gone.

The dance number ends as music and lights fade/cut.

FREYA *and* SONYA *on a bench, eating ice cream with takeaway coffees. It's a sunny day so they're wearing shades.*

In short, they look shit cool.

FREYA. Carbs and caffeine.

SONYA. The perfect combination.

Beat. They eat and drink.

I love autumn light. Slanty.

FREYA. Any sign?

SONYA. He said to meet at the gate. (*Signalling to nearby.*) I assumed he meant that one. Who knew this park has so many gates?

FREYA. If we stay put, he'll figure it out.

SONYA. I don't know. He's the one walking around with a cat box.

FREYA. True. However he managed it.

SONYA. He managed to surprise her all the way from Australia.

FREYA. He's some man.

SONYA. No wonder Loretta's always going on about him. He gave her a wonderful birthday. She was so happy on the phone, you should have heard her. I think it's a lovely story.

FREYA. You don't actually think he'll have Mary Robinson in that box?

SONYA. Why not? Cats get led astray. They get notions and join gangs. Especially when they're horny.

FREYA. She's neutered.

SONYA. Still. Wouldn't it be amazing? To be reunited after all this time.

FREYA. And if it's not her? We'll take whatever he's got, right?

SONYA. You want to?

FREYA. If you want to...

Beat.

SONYA. I mean, you're feeling up to the responsibility? If it's not Mary Robinson, she could be fairly wild.

FREYA. Since when has that ever stopped us.

SONYA. You're going through a lot at the moment. That's all I mean.

FREYA (*insistent*). I'm contesting the diagnosis.

SONYA. I know.

FREYA. I don't accept it. What do they know?

They were going off Dad's recollections, for Christ's sake.

SONYA. And the interviews.

FREYA. Yes and the... [interviews –] So what, you agree with them?

SONYA. What?

FREYA. You agree I'm –

SONYA. Why do you always do that?

FREYA. Do what?

SONYA. Pit me against you.

FREYA. No I don't.

SONYA. Oh, okay then.

FREYA. But I don't.

SONYA. All right!

Beat.

FREYA. And you shouldn't say 'always'.

SONYA. I know.

FREYA. 'Always' or 'never'. We swore off those.

SONYA. Yes. Sorry.

FREYA. Where is this guy?

Pause. The food and drink is finished.

SONYA. I didn't throw you out. Y'know?

Beat.

You left. You packed a bag and went home.

You always act like I ended it.

FREYA. You wouldn't let me come back.

SONYA. After a full week of not hearing from you.

FREYA. You could have called.

SONYA. Why? To see if you were okay? What about me? What if I wasn't okay?

FREYA. You feel empowered now, is that it? Now you know you didn't dump someone / with a – [disability?]

SONYA. I'm just saying you chose to go. At the time. You left me.

FREYA. If that's what you need to believe.

You were fairly clear when I came to collect my things, remember that conversation. I think we both know who did the dumping.

SONYA (*noticing something*). Oh my god!

FREYA. What?

SONYA. Is that your dad?

The sunglasses come off fully now, if they haven't before, or they're used to hide.

FREYA. Where?

SONYA. Over there. With the hot dog.

FREYA. What's he doing here?

SONYA. Well it's the weekend in the park on a sunny day. And it's a fairly popular food market so... I suppose it was bound to happen.

FREYA. Where is this guy with our cat?

SONYA. He's seen us.

FREYA. Dad?

SONYA. He's coming over.

FREYA. Well don't wave!

SONYA. What?

You have to face him at some point, Frey.

TONY *enters with an Italian sausage in a bun. Beat.*

TONY. I love their Italian sausages. Do you want one?

SONYA. We just had ice cream. Hi Tony. I'm not being rude, but we're here to meet someone and I have to check they're not waiting at the far gate.

FREYA. Don't go.

SONYA. Talk to your dad.

SONYA *moves to exit.*

TONY (*to* SONYA). You might run into Helen and Jack on your travels. They're around somewhere. With Colette.

SONYA. Right. Sure. I'll keep an eye out.

FREYA. I'll go with you.

SONYA. No. Stay.

SONYA *leaves. Awkward beat.*

TONY. We were running late. Gary has to pick up Jack so, I let them hop out while I looked for parking and well – (*Re: the hot dog.*) I love these things. I was going to find them after.

FREYA. Instead you found me.

TONY. How do you like that?

You sure you don't want one?

FREYA. How is Jack? How's it all going with him?

TONY. Teethmarks. On all his toys. Not a good sign apparently. Did you bite your toys?

FREYA. All babies do.

TONY. Yeah but Jack's four. Should have stopped by now. We don't know if the marks are recent. So we've given him a new train set. We'll see.

FREYA. You don't know yet?

TONY. It's a process, Helen says. Everything's a process. (*A new thought.*) Why, do you?

FREYA*'s face admits she has.*

The verdict is in. Well? Are we terrible parents?

FREYA. What?

TONY. Helen said she got you the number of a psychiatrist.

FREYA. Not a psychiatrist.

TONY. Whatever. Did you go see him? What did he say?

FREYA. I went to a psychologist. And it's a 'she'.

TONY. Oh right.

FREYA. And no.

TONY. No, what? No result?

Beat.

FREYA. I'm neuronormative, if you can believe that.

TONY. You're not on the spectrum?

I suppose we all are to some degree.

FREYA. No. We're not. That's a common misapprehension and it's an unhelpful one. There is a spectrum and while it's a wide spectrum, you're still very much on it or you're not on it and, apparently... I'm very much not on it.

TONY. Serious?

FREYA. Serious.

TONY. There's a turn-up for the books.

FREYA. Yeah.

TONY. You're sure now?

FREYA. I was thinking of contesting it.

TONY. What?

Beat.

FREYA. I'm sure.

TONY. So your mother and I – ?

FREYA. Are off the hook, yeah.

TONY. Well I wouldn't say that.

FREYA. Mam was right all along. You weren't so sure.

TONY. I don't know how she could have been. You were always... particular, you don't mind me saying. But your mother was convinced. We had words about it.

FREYA. Well she can lord it over both of us then.

TONY (*with conviction*). Freya, she'd never do that.

FREYA *is unconvinced.*

FREYA. So Mam's here?

TONY. Somewhere. She'll be all right though. Give her some time.

Pause.

You were giggling.

FREYA. What?

TONY. That night. The pair of you were giggling. But it was only meant to be Sonya in there so I was worried she was upset or –

That's why I looked in on you. On Sonya. You were making noise and I could hear it from the hallway.

Beat.

FREYA. Oh.

TONY. Yeah.

Beat.

It took about a week to remember that. Jesus.

I couldn't tell your mother what you said – and I tell your mother everything. But I couldn't tell her that.

If she entertained the idea for a millisecond, Freya. Even putting it out there... once an idea like that takes hold.

Beat.

I had to ask Helen to keep it to herself, y'know? Humiliating. And I'd say to myself, what are you ashamed about, you didn't do anything. And I don't know, I don't know if it was because we might have missed something, or maybe I felt like I didn't know you at all and who do I blame for that, only myself?

FREYA. I'm sorry, Daddy.

TONY. Did I ever give you a reason – [to think that of me?] Did I do something to you?

FREYA. I don't know. I don't know.

TONY. You were angry with me? You think I wasn't on your side, maybe.

FREYA. Not you – everybody!

Beat.

I'm angry with everybody.

TONY. Why?

FREYA. Look around!

TONY. Yeah, what? People enjoying their afternoon. Is that a problem?

FREYA. I don't mean... You refuse to understand anything.

TONY. And you sound like a teenager.

FREYA. Yeah well...

Beat.

The world is a fucked-up place. It's on fire.

TONY. And you like to point it out. Even though we can all see it.

FREYA. I don't like it. I don't like it. I don't want to always be... this low-lying rage under everything. No. I don't like it.

Beat.

TONY. This world. Feels like it's moving faster, the older I'm getting.

And I know I disappoint you.

FREYA *shakes her head.*

I've been wrong on a lot of things, I know that. And maybe that's why you have kids, so they can set you straight – maybe that's part of it.

But I heard you two laughing or sniggering or something and it was late and you were meant to be in the other room so I investigated and that's all there was to it.

FREYA. Sure, Dad. Of course. Makes sense.

Beat.

I don't know what's wrong with me.

And now... we're adopting a cat.

TONY. You what now?

FREYA. We're getting a cat.

TONY. You and Sonya?

FREYA. A new one. And I should feel great about it. I should feel great that I'm – that I'm not – I'm moving forward, y'know? We're…

Beat.

TONY. Getting a cat?

FREYA. Yeah!

(*Indicating.*) See the far side of the park? That man talking to Sonya? There's a ginger one in the box.

TONY. Like Mary Robinson.

FREYA. Very like Mary Robinson.

TONY. But it's not her?

Beat.

FREYA. No.

Pause.

So that's it. It's the way I am and I've no excuse.

TONY. For what?

FREYA. For being this unhappy.

Pause.

TONY. You back working?

FREYA. Dad.

TONY. You planning to?

You worked hard for that job.

FREYA. I will go back. Honest.

TONY. Look, I've watched you these last years. Campaigning, protesting, putting up with the likes of me. Gobshites who don't think before they give an opinion. And you always arguing back, like your life depended on it.

FREYA. Because it does.

TONY. Does it though? Cos there might be a cost to that. Don't you think?

See, I blame the new technologies. You don't get a break from it. Back in the day you'd go home, close the door and you escaped. All the politics and strife – left outside. Relief!

FREYA. I'm tired, Daddy. I'm tired. I don't want to keep fighting.

TONY. So... don't.

FREYA. I don't know how.

> COLETTE *and* HELEN *enter.* FREYA *straightens up.* HELEN *has Indian food while* COLETTE *has a cheese crêpe. Awkward pause.* COLETTE *is purse-lipped.*

No Jack?

HELEN. Gary's taken him off.

COLETTE. I thought he'd let him run around in the playground for a bit.

HELEN. He had plans.

COLETTE. On a Sunday afternoon?

HELEN. People make plans, even on Sundays.

COLETTE. I thought with the playground right there. The child could see it. It's like teasing him.

HELEN. Did Jack seem unhappy to you?

COLETTE. No.

HELEN. Well then.

TONY. You went for a crêpe?

COLETTE (*it sounded rude*). Excuse me? Oh yes. A savoury one.

TONY. So will I get us something sweet?

FREYA. Not for me.

COLETTE. Do. And a tea?

TONY. Helen?

HELEN. I'm fine with my samosa, thanks.

TONY. Grand, grand. Be right back.

TONY exits. Another awkward pause.

FREYA. I had an ice cream already.

Beat.

COLETTE. Did we see Sonya talking to some man?

FREYA. She'll be back soon. She knows where I am.

Beat.

So Gary took Jack then?

COLETTE. He's been very good, hasn't he, Helen?

HELEN. Since when?

COLETTE. Since Jack's difficulty.

HELEN. Please don't describe it that way.

And what do you mean, very good?

COLETTE. Well he's been reliable, hasn't he? And sensitive to Jack's needs.

HELEN. He was always that.

COLETTE. Well that's what I mean.

HELEN. He's his father, Mam.

COLETTE. I don't know what you expect. I've noticed a real change in him.

HELEN. In Gary?

COLETTE. Since the news.

HELEN. Right.

COLETTE. What has your goat?

HELEN. Nothing.

COLETTE. Is this for Freya's benefit?

HELEN. What?

COLETTE (*to* FREYA). I don't know why she's being like this.

FREYA. Like what?

HELEN. Yeah, Mam, like what?

COLETTE. I'm only saying Gary has been very good at looking after Jack.

HELEN. For the two days a week he has to.

COLETTE. Whatever.

HELEN. But it's not whatever, is it? It's forever.

COLETTE. We were having a lovely day, Freya. I'm not sure where this is coming from.

HELEN. It's from you eulogising Gary for doing fuck-all.

COLETTE. Language, Helen.

HELEN. Look, Gary's been fine. But I'm the one dealing with the school. I'm the one making sure Gary is thinking ahead when he arranges things for Jack. I'm looking after all the appointments. Keeping track of Jack's mood diary. Doing the special classes.

COLETTE. I thought Gary went with you.

HELEN. Because I told him to. I did the research. Figured it out – enrolled us! He just had to show up. I sent him a map pin, for Christ's sake.

COLETTE. Well what do you want, a medal?

HELEN. Yes please. Someone give me a medal. Or a plaque. Child Manager of the Month. Best Personal Secretary to two children: Jack – my son – and Gary, the man-child who knocked me up and who I, mistaking enthusiastic commitment for actual responsibility (and not for the first time) went and married. What award do I get for that?

Beat. COLETTE *looks to share her surprise at this outburst with* FREYA, *no success.*

COLETTE. Look, it's unfortunate –

HELEN. It's not unfortunate. Please stop saying that.

COLETTE. – but we're just going to have to roll with it.

FREYA. Roll with it?

COLETTE. That's right. Whatever happens.

Beat.

HELEN. Fine!

Pause.

FREYA. I'm sorry I haven't been available to you, Helen.

COLETTE. Have you not?

FREYA. But I will be. From now on.

HELEN. Did you sort things out with Dad?

FREYA. Think so. Just now.

HELEN. Did you apologise?

FREYA nods.

COLETTE. Sort what out?

FREYA. Nothing.

Beat. COLETTE *looks to* HELEN.

COLETTE. Fine then. Don't tell me.

Beat.

FREYA (*to* COLETTE). I got your voice note.

Beat.

HELEN. What voice note?

FREYA. You know how Mam hates texting?

HELEN. Oh, right.

FREYA. Anyway. I got it.

COLETTE. Well... that's fine then.

FREYA. Is it?

Beat.

COLETTE. Do you have a napkin, Helen?

HELEN. Yeah, here.

ACT THREE   85

COLETTE. Thank you.

FREYA. Fine.

    TONY *arrives back with a tea and a bun, which he shares with* COLETTE.

TONY. Here we are.

COLETTE. Thanks, Tony.

TONY. You're sure you didn't want something, Helen?

HELEN. Actually, I'm gonna head on.

TONY. We'll drop you some place.

HELEN. No I'll take a walk. Some alone time. While Gary has Jack.

TONY. You sure?

    SONYA *enters, empty-handed*.

SONYA (*slightly awkward and forced, to whole group*). Hi.

HELEN. Oh Sonya, I was about to head off. All okay with you?

SONYA. Huh?… Yeah. All good.

HELEN. Work still… working out?

COLETTE. Oh you've a new job, did I hear?

SONYA. I do, Colette. It's going well, thanks.

HELEN. Great. Well, I'll see you again.

SONYA. Yeah, sure. See ya, Helen.

FREYA. Bye, Hels. And Helen?

    HELEN *stops*.

    I'll call you. I promise.

HELEN. Do.

    HELEN *exits*.

COLETTE. We can't stay much longer either, can we, Tone? I'm doing the rota for meals on wheels and I've to make a bunch of calls.

SONYA. It's good to see you.

COLETTE. And you, Sonya. You know how fond we are of you.

(*To* FREYA.) Be good to this one. You're lucky to have her.

Beat.

And we should all catch up. Maybe next Sunday? I'll do a roast.

TONY. Will you?

COLETTE. Might as well. Helen has Jack next weekend.

TONY. Oh, right then. Next Sunday so.

(*To* SONYA.) You didn't take the cat then?

SONYA. What?

TONY. Adopt it, or whatever?

SONYA. Oh, no. No, it wasn't ours. I mean, it wasn't for us.

TONY. Ah that's a shame. But if it isn't for you... [it won't pass you by.]

COLETTE. Come on, Tony.

TONY. Right.

Oh I finished that job, on the Ford Consul. Looking great now. It hasn't been picked up so... some evening, if you wanted that spin? Freya could drive. Only if you're interested. You'll let me know.

COLETTE *and* TONY *exit. Beat.* SONYA *drops the act.*

SONYA. It wasn't her.

FREYA. No?

SONYA *cries, shaking her head.* FREYA *holds her.*

Oh I'm sorry, Son.

SONYA. I tried to bond with her. I really did, cos she looked so [like her...] uncanny. She had her ears and her long, elegant paws?

SONYA *crosses her hands like a cat.* FREYA *smiles.*

But it wasn't her.

FREYA. No Mary McAleese for us then?

SONYA *shakes her head, taking out a tissue.*

SONYA. There's only one Mary Robinson. We couldn't replace her. Remember how she'd purr when you pulled on her neck?

FREYA (*a shared dad jok*e). She was purr-fect.

SONYA *smiles. Beat.*

SONYA. She was.

FREYA. I'm sorry, Sonya.

SONYA *recovers a little.*

SONYA. We have a dinner invitation?

FREYA. We do.

SONYA. So everything's…?

FREYA. Brushed under the carpet, in true Pattison-family style.

SONYA. They've always been nice to me.

FREYA. They prefer you actually.

SONYA. Yeah. I think they do.

FREYA (*slightly taken aback*). All right then!

SONYA. No I do.

I was so in awe of them. How they handled everything. How open and kind they were, how generous they were with me. I'd talk to Colette, you know? About Mam. About everything really. And she'd listen. And I was only a teenager.

But now I think…

FREYA. What?

SONYA. Helen said to me once… 'We like you. You're good for Freya.'

FREYA (*mock offended*). [Patronising] Wagon.

SONYA. ...But at the time... It was around you moving in with me and I took it as a compliment. They were entrusting me with you. To look after you.

But now I think... I was taking you off their hands.

FREYA. Are you okay, Son?

SONYA. They're still good people. I'm not saying... But they were relieved, a little. To pass you on to me. Because I was there, they didn't have to worry about you.

FREYA. I was the one looking after you.

SONYA. Oh I know. I know you were. But from their perspective...

FREYA (*playfully*). You're not making any sense.

SONYA. No?

FREYA *shakes her head. Pause.*

FREYA. Let's go home.

SONYA. You told Tony we were adopting a cat?

Beat.

Why didn't you tell him it was Mary Robinson?

FREYA. What do you mean?

SONYA. You didn't tell him it might be her?

FREYA. No.

SONYA. Why not?

FREYA. Because... I'm sorry, Sonya, but Mary Robinson is dead. (*Gently.*) We know this.

SONYA. You know it.

Beat.

How do you?

I thought you were looking out for me. With Loretta. All those exhausting phone calls.

FREYA. I'm still not sure about Loola.

SONYA. But after they found her? Once there definitely was a cat... that photo! It could have been Mary Robinson.

FREYA. Oh yeah. Sure.

SONYA. She looked identical.

FREYA. Absolutely.

SONYA. But you didn't say it might be her. You told Tony we were adopting.

Why would you do that? Why wouldn't you just... you were so convinced?

FREYA. I didn't think... it would be her.

SONYA. You knew it wouldn't be. How did you know?

FREYA. It's been so long, Sonya.

SONYA (*with conviction*). But it could have been her. Why wouldn't you say...? It would have been amazing.

FREYA. Yeah, of course, exactly! It was never going to be Mary Robinson.

SONYA (*frustrated*). Why not?

FREYA. It just wasn't. Now can we go?

SONYA. What do you know, Freya? What are you not telling me?

Beat.

You know something.

FREYA. I don't.

SONYA. I know when you're lying. Are you lying to me?

FREYA. Sonya!

SONYA. You are lying! How did you know it wasn't Mary Robinson? (*Vehemently.*) Freya, how did you know?

FREYA. Because I killed her!

Beat.

SONYA. What?

FREYA. Sonya –

SONYA. What did you say?

FREYA. It was an accident. I didn't *kill her* kill her – I didn't mean to.

Beat.

That night I came by the flat. You wouldn't see me and well, Mary Robinson was outside. Patrolling the perimeter. And you refused to buzz me up, so –

SONYA. Oh god.

FREYA. I took her. I took her in the car.

SONYA. Where?

FREYA. Mam and Dad's. I was going to look after her for a bit... But she fucking hates the car. So taking her out – she wasn't herself – she scratched me. I dropped her. In the driveway. And she set off...

SONYA. Oh Frey.

FREYA. I think she was on her way back to the flat. But she bolted... I tried to follow her, I tried to keep up... but she went round this corner and I heard a car screech and...

Beat.

It was all my fault.

Beat.

I couldn't tell you, Sonya. I'm sorry, I'm so sorry.

I felt terrible. But you weren't talking to me so...

SONYA. So you said nothing?

FREYA. I think I started to blame you. If you had only... talked to me. Let me see you. You were stubborn, Sonya!

Beat.

And time passed. And then you showed up after Loretta called and –

ACT THREE 91

SONYA (*realising what happened*). No. No, because... I put out flyers.

FREYA. Yeah I know.

SONYA. We talked on the phone.

FREYA. I couldn't tell you. That's why –

SONYA. I searched for days. I apologised to you. You blamed me.

FREYA. You dumped me!

SONYA. You let me think I lost her.

FREYA (*very upset but fighting it*). I know. I know I did.

SONYA. You could have said at any time.

FREYA. I couldn't though. I couldn't, Sonya. I'm sorry, really I am.

I love you.

SONYA. No. No, you don't get to say that.

FREYA. But I do, Sonya!

SONYA. You can't imagine your life without me, and that's not the same thing.

Beat.

It's sick. It's sick what you've done.

FREYA. I know.

SONYA. I can't forgive you for it.

FREYA. I know.

SONYA. I won't.

I won't, Freya.

FREYA. Okay.

SONYA. I'll blame you forever.

Beat.

FREYA (*nodding*). I deserve it, so...

SONYA *sits down.*

Pause.

What are we going to do?

Let's go home and talk about this properly.

Pause.

Let's not be that couple, Son [that argue in public]. We can talk at home.

SONYA. I don't want to go home.

FREYA (*frustrated*). Well we can't...

Beat.

Okay, all right then. Whatever you want.

They sit in silence. Pause.

I really do feel terrible.

SONYA. I believe you.

FREYA. I do, Sonya.

SONYA. You should.

Another pause.

You packed a bag. You left.

We had an argument and somehow it was my fault for getting upset.

FREYA. But that wasn't why [we broke up].

SONYA. You left me.

And it was the most shocking thing.

When you didn't call, for a full week?

FREYA. I don't know why I did that. I was... frustrated and I needed to get away, or.

SONYA. What about what I needed?

FREYA. Don't say that. Don't act like I didn't care about you. I loved you. I still love you. You're my world!

SONYA. Do you even like the world, Freya?

FREYA. Let's go home.

SONYA (*loudly*). I don't want to go home!

FREYA. Okay, all right!

Beat.

SONYA. It took the whole week to see it. To have the space to... [see it.]

Beat.

We were teenagers when we started. We didn't know what we were.

Still, we fought. We fought for our rights. We fought... for a long time, and I wouldn't have had the strength, without you. Cos we were only kids.

But now, you have a law degree. We changed the world, or this country at any rate. And I... even I have become an adult, somehow. And I'm so proud.

You showed me what to do. You led the way, Freya, and I will always love you for that. My warrior princess. I am proud of us.

But not these last months. Not this last year.

FREYA. But that isn't us. That's not really [us...] It's just a rut.

SONYA. I knew there was something wrong. Something deep down...

I thought there had to be a reason.

But there's no reason. It's just...

FREYA. / Unfair.

SONYA. Us. What?

FREYA. I did try though. I tried so hard.

Beat.

SONYA. I want your keys, Freya. To the flat.

FREYA. Sonya.

Beat.

But you love me.

Beat.

Sonya!?

What am I supposed to do? Where am I supposed to go?

I'll be better. I can be better. I just… I need something to change. That's all. Someone to listen. I need… I need you, Sonya! The way you needed me all those years.

SONYA. Your keys, Freya?

FREYA. Please, Sonya!?

I tried. I was trying.

I didn't know what you wanted from me… that's…

But we fixed it. We can fix it, Sonya. And now we definitely are that couple, so…

Talk to me… Sonya…

Pause.

…Okay.

FREYA *takes out her keys. She almost offers them but then takes them back.*

I have to get my car key off…

…and Mam and Dad's…

After some time, the keys are ready.

I really am so sorry, and I think, y'know, in time we could still –

Son. Sonya?… Look at me!

SONYA *looks at* FREYA.

ACT THREE

Please.

Please don't leave me.

I can change, I'll...

SONYA *snatches the keys and rises.*

No, no, Sonya... please, / Sonya!

SONYA *exits.* FREYA *is left alone. She paces, self-conscious. She sits. She looks after* SONYA. SONYA *is very gone.* FREYA *cries quietly, aware she's in public. Silence.* FREYA *takes out her phone, considers.* FREYA *dials.*

Heya. It's me.

Beat.

Are you still on your walk? I'm in the park and... well, I wanted to say something. When you married Gary, I was never disappointed in you. I want you to know that cos you said before I judged you for it, and well... I might have slagged you for having to repeat your exams cos that was hilarious but... But you were my big sister and I thought you were a boss, right? And I thought Gary was cool. Yeah, no, I don't any more, I think he's an a-hole now, but at the time... And I think being a mother is cool. Okay? I think you rock. And I don't know why you thought anything else cos I never said anything, so it must all be on you, okay? I wanted to tell you that, Hels.

Beat.

Right. That's all. I'll go now.

Beat.

Yeah, no I'm... good. Oh she's fine too, at least... she will be fine. What are we doing? Oh we were just going to... I don't know, we were about to... ehm...

Beat.

Well we broke up actually so...

Beat.

Yeah, no, we did. It's not good. Not good, no, not good at all.

Beat.

I'm – I don't know, coming apart, I think? I don't really...

Beat.

I'm in the park, yeah and there's all these... happy people and... Sonya's gone, Helen, she's... she left me.

Beat.

I don't know. I don't know.

Beat.

Yeah... yeah do. That'd be good. Only if it suits... you have enough on your... [plate] oh, okay then.

Beat.

I'll wait. Yeah, I won't go anywhere.

HELEN *enters from behind on her mobile. She sees* FREYA *from a distance.*

I'll wait for you. Thanks, Hels, thanks, I'll...

I'll just be here.

FREYA *hangs up. She waits.* HELEN *lowers her phone, watches.*

Lights out.

The End.

A Nick Hern Book

Sandpaper on Sunburn first published in Great Britain as a paperback original in 2024 by Nick Hern Books Limited, The Glasshouse, 49a Goldhawk Road, London W12 8QP, in association with Verdant Productions

Sandpaper on Sunburn copyright © 2024 David Horan

David Horan has asserted his right to be identified as the author of this work

Cover image: Ros Kavanagh

Designed and typeset by Nick Hern Books, London
Printed in Great Britain by Mimeo Ltd, Huntingdon, Cambridgeshire PE29 6XX

A CIP catalogue record for this book is available from the British Library

ISBN 978 1 83904 389 5

CAUTION All rights whatsoever in this play are strictly reserved. Requests to reproduce the text in whole or in part should be addressed to the publisher.

Performing Rights Applications for performance, including readings and excerpts, in any medium and in any language throughout the world, should be addressed, in the first instance, to the Performing Rights Manager, Nick Hern Books, The Glasshouse, 49a Goldhawk Road, London W12 8QP, *tel* +44 (0)20 8749 4953, *email* rights@nickhernbooks.co.uk, except as follows:

Australia: ORiGiN Theatrical, Level 1, 213 Clarence Street, Sydney NSW 2000, *tel* +61 (2) 8514 5201, *email* enquiries@originmusic.com.au, *web* www.origintheatrical.com.au

New Zealand: Play Bureau, 20 Rua Street, Mangapapa, Gisborne, 4010, *tel* +64 21 258 3998, *email* info@playbureau.com

No performance of any kind may be given unless a licence has been obtained. Applications should be made before rehearsals begin. Publication of this play does not necessarily indicate its availability for amateur performance.

www.nickhernbooks.co.uk/environmental-policy

www.nickhernbooks.co.uk

facebook.com/nickhernbooks
twitter.com/nickhernbooks